S E R I E S

A NavPress Bible study on the book of

MATTHEW

NAVPRESS
BRINGING TRUTH TO LIFE
NavPress Publishing Group
P.O. Box 35001, Colorado Springs, Colorado 80935

The Navigators is an international Christian organization. Our mission is to reach, disciple, and equip people to know Christ and to make Him known through successive generations. We envision multitudes of diverse people in the United States and every other nation who have a passionate love for Christ, live a lifestyle of sharing Christ's love, and multiply spiritual laborers among those without Christ.

NavPress is the publishing ministry of The Navigators. NavPress publications help believers learn biblical truth and apply what they learn to their lives and ministries. Our mission is to stimulate spiritual formation among our readers.

Printed in the United States of America

2 3 4 5 6 7 8 9 10 11 12 13 14 15 / 99

FOR A FREE CATALOG OF
NAVPRESS BOOKS & BIBLE STUDIES,
CALL 1-800-366-7788 (USA)
or 1-416-499-4615 (CANADA)

CONTENTS

ACKNOWLEDGMENTS

The LifeChange series has been produced through the coordinated efforts of Navigator Bible study developers and NavPress editorial staff, along with a nationwide network of fieldtesters.

AUTHOR: STEVE HALLIDAY
SERIES EDITOR: KAREN LEE-THORP

HOW TO USE THIS STUDY

This LIFECHANGE guide to the book of Matthew is designed to give students a good overview of the first Gospel. Although in the past century many critics have considered the Gospel of Mark to be more important textually than Matthew, it is hard to argue that any other Gospel has more profoundly influenced Christian thinking than Matthew. In fact, from the second century onward, this Gospel has been more frequently quoted than any other. Its distinctly Hebrew thought and emphasis on the fulfillment of Old Testament prophecies suggest it was created especially for Jewish believers, yet countless non-Jewish believers throughout the ages have been instructed, comforted, and encouraged by its timeless message.

Objectives

Although LIFECHANGE guides vary with the individual books they explore, they share some common goals:

1. To provide you with a firm foundation of understanding and a thirst to return to each book;
2. To teach you by example how to study a book of the Bible without structured guides;
3. To give you all the historical background, word definitions, and explanatory notes you need, so that your only other reference is the Bible;
4. To help you grasp the message of each book as a whole;
5. To teach you how to let God's Word transform you into Christ's image.

Each lesson in this study is designed to take 60 to 90 minutes to complete on your own. The guide is based on the assumption that you are completing one lesson per week, but if time is limited you can do half a lesson per week or whatever amount allows you to be thorough.

5

Flexibility

LIFECHANGE guides are flexible, allowing you to adjust the quantity and depth of your study to meet your individual needs. The guide offers many optional questions in addition to the regular numbered questions. The optional questions, which appear in the margins of the study pages, include the following:

Optional Application. Nearly all application questions are optional; we hope you will do as many as you can without overcommitting yourself.

For Thought and Discussion. Beginning Bible students should be able to handle these questions, but even advanced students need to think about them. These questions frequently deal with ethical issues and other biblical principles. They often offer cross-references to spark thought, but the references do not contain obvious answers. These questions are good for group discussions.

For Further Study. These questions include: (a) cross-references that shed light on a topic the book discusses, and (b) questions that delve deeper into the passage. You can omit them to shorten a lesson without missing a major point of the passage.

If you are meeting in a group, decide together which optional questions to prepare for each lesson and how much of the lesson you will cover at the next meeting. Normally, the group leader should make this decision, but you might let each member choose his or her own application questions.

Sometimes there is space in the margins of the study guide to jot answers to optional question or notes from your discussion. You will often want more space for such notes, however. You can use blank pages between lessons and at the end of the guide for notes, or you can begin a separate Bible study notebook. A separate notebook will give you plenty of room to answer optional questions, record prayer requests and answers to prayer, write notes from discussions, plan applications and record results, and describe experiences in your life that are teaching you spiritual lessons. A notebook like this can be invaluable.

As you grow in your walk with God, you will find the LIFECHANGE guide growing with you—a helpful reference on a topic, a continuing challenge for application, a source of questions for many levels of growth.

Overview and details

This guide begins with an overview of Matthew. The key to interpretation is context—what is the whole passage or book *about*? And the key to context is purpose—what is the author's *aim* for the whole work? In the first lesson you will lay the foundation for your study by asking yourself, "Why did the author (and God) write the book? What did they want to accomplish? What is the book about?"

Then over the next seventeen lessons, you will analyze successive passages in detail. You'll interpret particular verses in light of what the whole paragraph is about, and paragraphs in light of the whole passage. You'll consider how each passage contributes to the total message of the book. (Frequently reviewing an outline of the book will enable you to make these connections.) Then, once you understand what the passage says, you'll apply it to your own life.

In lesson eighteen, you will review what Jesus revealed about His own and the disciples' missions in the world and the whole Gospel, returning to the big picture to see whether your view of it has changed after closer study. Review will also strengthen your grasp of major issues and give you an idea of how you have grown from your study.

Kinds of questions

Bible study on your own—without a structured guide—follows a progression. First you observe: What does the passage *say*? Then you interpret: What does the passage *mean*? Lastly you apply: How does this truth *affect* my life?

Some of the "how" and "why" questions will take some creative thinking, even prayer, to answer. Some are opinion questions without clear-cut, right-or-wrong answers; these will lend themselves to discussions and side studies.

Don't let your study become an exercise in knowledge alone. Treat the passage as God's Word, and stay in dialogue with Him as you study. Pray, "Lord, what do you want me to see here?" "Father, why is this true?" "Lord, how does this apply to my life?"

It is important that you write down your answers. The act of writing clarifies your thinking and helps you remember.

Study aids

A list of reference materials, including a few notes of explanation to help you make good use of them, begins on page 199. This guide is designed to include enough background to let you interpret with just your Bible and the guide. Still, if you want more information on a subject or want to study a book on your own, try the references listed.

Scripture versions

Unless otherwise indicated, the Bible quotations in this guide are from the New International Version of the Bible. Other versions cited are the Revised Standard Version (RSV), the New American Standard Bible (NASB), and the King James Version (KJV).

Use any translation you like for study, preferably more than one. A paraphrase, such as *The Message*, is not suitable for study, but it can be helpful for comparison or devotional reading.

Memorizing and meditating

The psalmist wrote, "I have hidden your word in my heart that I might not sin against you" (Psalm 119:11). If you write down a verse or passage that challenges or encourages you, and reflect on it often for a week or more, you will find it

7

beginning to affect your motives and actions. We forget quickly what we read once; we remember what we ponder.

When you find a significant verse or passage, you might copy it onto a card to keep with you. Set aside five minutes during each day just to think about what the passage might mean in your life. Recite it over to yourself, exploring its meaning. Then, return to your passage as often as you can during the day for a brief review. You will soon find it coming to mind spontaneously.

Why group study?

What is the benefit of studying in a group? Two reasons come immediately to mind: *accountability* and *support*. When members commit to the rest of the group to seek growth in an area of life, you can pray with one another, listen jointly for God's guidance, help one another resist temptation, assure each other that the other's growth matters to you, use the group to practice spiritual principles, and so on.

A group of four to ten people allows the richest discussions, but you can adapt this guide for groups of other sizes. It will suit a wide range of group types, such as home Bible studies, growth groups, youth groups, and workplace studies. Both new and experienced Bible students, as well as new and mature Christians, will benefit from this guide. You can omit or leave for later any questions you find too easy or too hard.

This guide is designed to lead a group through one lesson per week, but feel free to split lessons if you want to discuss them more thoroughly. Or, omit some questions in a lesson if preparation or discussion time is limited. You can always return to this guide for personal study later on. You will be able to discuss only a few questions at length, so choose some for discussion and others for background. Make time at each discussion for members to ask about anything that gave them trouble.

Each lesson in the guide ends with a section called "For the group." These sections give advice on how to focus a discussion, how you might apply the lesson in your group, how to pray about what you've learned, and so on. The group leader should read each "For the group" at least a week ahead so that he or she can tell the group how to prepare for the next lesson.

Each member should prepare for a meeting by writing answers for all the background and discussion questions to be covered. If the group decides not to take an hour per week for private preparation, then expect to take at least two meetings per lesson to work through the questions. Application will be very difficult, however, without private thought and prayer.

If you write down each other's applications and prayer requests, you are more likely to remember to pray for them during the week, to ask about them at the next meeting, and to notice answered prayers. You might want to add a section for prayer requests in your Bible study notebook.

Notes taken during discussion will help you remember, follow up on ideas, stay on the subject, and clarify a total view of an issue. But don't let note taking keep you from participating. Some groups choose one member at each meeting to take notes. Then someone copies the notes and distributes them at the next meeting. Share these tasks so that everyone will feel included and no one will feel burdened. Some groups have someone take notes on a large pad of paper or erasable marker board (preformed shower wallboard works well), so that everyone can see what has been recorded. Others have someone take notes on a laptop computer, then print out the results at the end of the meeting.

Structuring your group time

The following scheme suggests one possible way to structure your discussions. Adapt these suggestions in whatever way best suits your group.

Worship. Begin with prayer and/or singing. Some pray only briefly for God's guidance at the beginning, leaving extended prayer until after the study.

Warm-up. Profitable studies early on lay a good foundation for honest sharing of ideas, getting comfortable with each other, and encouraging a sense of common purpose. One way to establish common ground is to talk about what each group member hopes to get out of the study and out of any prayer, singing, outreach, or anything else you might do together. You might also discuss what you hope to give to the group. Write down each member's hopes and expectations, so later you can look back at these goals to see if they are being met. You can then plan more time for prayer or decide to move more deliberately through the study.

Take some time at the outset to talk about goals. Some groups use one session to hand out study guides, introduce the study, examine the "How to Use This Study" section on pages 5-10, and discuss goals.

Discussion. You may find it helpful to discuss each member's first impressions as you progress through the study. What was most helpful? Did anything startle you? What questions do you have? What overall impression did you gain from the session?

To focus your discussion, you might ask each group member to choose one scene or teaching that was especially meaningful to him or her, then explain why. This open discussion often helps members to get to know one another better.

Study. Follow the study guidelines in whatever manner best helps you to grasp the meaning of the biblical text. Your overarching goal should be to gain a thorough understanding of the passage under review.

Application. The last step of Bible study is asking yourself, "What difference should this passage make in my life? How should it make me want to think or act?" Application will require time, thought, prayer, and perhaps discussion with someone else.

At times, you may find it most productive to concentrate on one specific application, giving it careful thought and prayer. At other times you may want to list several implications a passage of Scripture has for your life, and then choose one to focus on for prayer and action. Use whatever method helps you to grow more obedient to God's Word.

Some possible applications for a passage: "I need to ask God for the ability and discipline to obey by His Spirit." "I need to stop . . . " "I need to ask the Holy Spirit to help me . . ." "I believe I should . . ."

As you develop applications, remember that we must cooperate with God if we are to grow spiritually; both we and God have a part to play (Philippians 2:12-13). Effective application must be saturated with prayer for guidance, ability, forgiveness, discipline, encouragement, etc.

9

If application is unfamiliar to some group members, choose a sample paragraph from the Gospel and discuss possible ways of applying it. Try to state specifically how the passage is relevant to you and how you might act in light of it. Think of responses that you might actually make, not merely ideal responses. Don't neglect prayer for ability, courage, discipline, and guidance to carry out the response you have identified!

Give the group a chance to voice any questions about the passages under review or historical/cultural references that may puzzle them. You may decide to postpone answering some questions until you have access to appropriate information. It's a good idea to write them down in order to keep them in mind as the study progresses.

Wrap-up. The wrap-up is a time to bring the discussion to a focused end and to make any announcements about the next lesson or meeting. Most of the lessons in this study cover more than one chapter of the Gospel; your group may decide to tackle some of these lessons in more than one session. Make sure you decide ahead of time how much of each lesson you plan to study at your next session.

Prayer. Praise God for His wisdom in giving us the teachings, principles, inspiration, and encouragement found in the Gospel of Matthew. Praise Him for what He reveals about Himself in this book and ask Him to teach you to know, love, and obey Him throughout your study of Matthew.

Beyond these suggestions, pages 201-202 lists some good sources of counsel for leading group studies.

BACKGROUND

Matthew and His Gospel

A Gospel

Gospel is an Old English word that means "good news." It is a translation of the Greek word *euangelion* (*eu-*, "good" and *angelion*, "message"), and gives us words like "evangelist," and is related to words like "angel."

When the first Christians wanted to record the "good news" about the Man who was God, none of the familiar forms of literature seemed suitable. The Christians didn't write the kinds of autobiographies or sacred texts that were common in the current Greek, Roman, or Jewish culture. Instead, they created a new form: the Gospel.

The Gospels are composed of scenes and sayings from Jesus' life remembered by His disciples and passed on, probably word for word. As Leon Morris notes, "Rabbis used to cast their teaching into forms suitable for memorization and insist that their pupils learn it by heart."[1] The apostles faithfully recalled both individual statements and the overall progress of Jesus' time with them.

While Matthew's Gospel certainly reflects these general characteristics, it is unique in many ways. It "vividly sets forth the evidence that Jesus of Nazareth, of Davidic descent, is the Messiah promised in the Old Testament, the expected King of the Jews."[2] With its emphasis on the fulfillment of Old Testament prophecies, it forms a natural bridge between the Old Testament and the New. The word "kingdom" appears in this Gospel some fifty-six times, more than any other; the unique phrase "kingdom of heaven" is used thirty-two times in Matthew but nowhere else. Matthew alone quotes Jesus' reference to "the throne of his glory" (19:28, 25:31) and calls Jerusalem "the holy city" (4:5) and "the city of the Great King" (5:35).[3]

Yet Matthew never has been a book for Jewish readers alone. From the visit of the Magi reported at the beginning of this Gospel to the words of the Great Commission at its conclusion, the larger sphere and interests of the Messiah are clear. Only Matthew includes a parable in which Jesus predicts that unbelieving Israel would be supplanted by others. And only Matthew, of all the Gospels, mentions the church (16:18, 18:17).

11

Four Gospels

Many collections of Jesus' words and deeds were composed in the first century after His death, but God uniquely inspired four men to write the Gospels that would bear His authority. Why four? We can speculate, or we can simply be glad for all four masterful portraits that reveal our Lord in different lights. As J. Sidlow Baxter asks, which of the four could we do without?[4]

It is striking how such a picture of a single man and a single set of events emerges from four such different points of view. Observe the distinct interests and emphases in these examples:

1. To Matthew, who writes for Jewish Christians, Jesus is, above all, the King of David's line promised in the Hebrew Scriptures and the Teacher who brings a new revelation of God's Law. Matthew weaves fulfillments of Old Testament prophecies around five discourses about the Law and the Kingdom. Mark pens a short Gospel in quick scenes that drive toward the cross, revealing Christ more in works of power and service than in words of wisdom. Luke crafts his account of the Son of Man, the Savior of the world, to be meticulously accurate and also captivating for a cultured Greek audience. And John records a few miraculous signs and several long discourses to spark faith in God the Son.
2. John begins with Jesus' pre-existence as God, and Mark starts with Jesus' baptism as an adult. Neither tells of Jesus' birth or lineage. Matthew opens with a genealogy that traces from Abraham (the father of the Israelite covenant) to David (the head of the Jewish royal line) and finally to Joseph (Jesus' legal father in Jewish eyes, though not His natural one). Matthew's birth account focuses on kingship and prophecy, while Luke narrates the birth with warm, human touches. Luke also traces Jesus back to Adam — the father of Jew and Gentile alike — and then to God. But while Matthew's Jewish-minded nativity focuses on men, Luke delights in pregnant women and widows.
3. John highlights Jesus' ministry in Jerusalem. Matthew and Mark describe mainly His Galilean ministry and His last week in Jerusalem. Luke includes ten long chapters in which Jesus journeys toward Jerusalem, training His disciples. We call Matthew, Mark, and Luke the synoptic (one view) Gospels because they have much more material in common than any of them has with John.

Throughout this study of Matthew's Gospel, more features that mark Matthew's unique contribution to Scripture will be noted.

The author of Matthew

Early church tradition unanimously ascribes this book to the apostle Matthew. In fact, all early manuscripts of this Gospel feature the superscription "according to Matthew" and there is no evidence that it ever circulated without this heading.[5]

While it is true this title was not originally part of the manuscript, there is good reason to believe it was affixed no later than A.D. 125—and if so, it is clear the church had settled on Matthew's authorship well before that date.

The church father Papias (ca. A.D. 150), bishop of Hierapolis, provides the earliest external testimony that Matthew was the author of the Gospel which bears his name. Papias wrote (somewhat enigmatically), "Matthew therefore wrote the oracles in the Hebrew dialect, and every one interpreted them as he was able."[6] Irenaeus (ca. A.D. 185), Origen (ca. A.D. 185–254), and Eusebius (ca. A.D. 324) all name Matthew as the author of this Gospel.

Many modern critics, however, doubt the early church's universal belief in Matthean authorship. Citing several difficulties suggested by a few commonly accepted synoptic source hypotheses, they prefer to leave the question of authorship open. Yet noted New Testament authority Donald Guthrie concludes, "It may be said that there is no conclusive reason for rejecting the strong external testimony regarding the authorship of Matthew."[7]

What do we know of the biblical Matthew? He was also called Levi and was the son of Alphaeus (Mark 2:14). An employee at the toll house in Capernaum, he either worked directly for Herod Antipas or under someone who had the taxes of the district in tenure. After he responded to Jesus' call, Matthew "held a great banquet for Jesus at his house" (Luke 5:29). He is listed as one of the twelve apostles chosen by Jesus (Mark 3:13-19; Luke 6:12-16) and is last named in Acts 1:13 as one of the twelve in the upper room after Jesus' ascension. Beyond that, we know almost nothing of him.

When did Matthew write?

The date of Matthew's composition is debated and remains largely conjectural. There are few internal indications of its probable date, and even the few that exist can be (and have been) interpreted in various ways.

Hiebert says the two occurrences of "unto this day" (27:8; 28:15) show "a considerable lapse of time between the events recorded and the time of writing," yet writes that "the statement in 27:8, 'Wherefore that field was called, The field of blood, unto this day,' naturally points to a date before A.D. 70," since after the destruction of Jerusalem the field would no longer be so identified or used.[8] He therefore suggests a date for Matthew between A.D. 66 and 68.

Guthrie prefers to leave the date "undetermined," suggesting that those who opt for a date between A.D. 80 and 100 do so primarily because of disbelief in the possibility of predictive prophecy (which Matthew 24 contains).

After a thorough discussion of the dating possibilities, D. A. Carson writes that "while surprisingly little in the Gospel conclusively points to a firm date, perhaps the sixties are the most likely decade for its composition." And R. A. Nixon in *The New Bible Commentary: Revised* sums up the main possibilities when he concludes, "It is wiser . . . to say that Matthew should be dated somewhere between A.D. 65 and 110, with the Jewish nature of the Gospel and its many parallels with the Dead Sea Scrolls suggesting a date well within the first half of the period."[9]

13

Why did Matthew write?

While every Gospel aims at an accurate portrayal of Christ in order to inspire faith in its readers, each Gospel features a few unique emphases. Matthew was written primarily for a Jewish audience, both as an apologetic against unbelieving Jews and as a tool to deepen the believer's understanding of and devotion to the Messiah.

More than any other Gospel, Matthew has a well-developed underlying structure, alternating five discourse sections with narrative sections. For this reason, it is especially well-suited for teaching. Nixon supplies a very helpful summary:

> We may conclude that the Gospel was probably written by a Jewish Christian for Jewish Christians in close contact with unbelieving Jews somewhere near to Palestine in the latter part of the first century A.D. It was intended to instruct them carefully in the way in which Jesus had fulfilled the prophecies of the Old Testament and had laid the foundations of the Christian church, continuous with the people of God in the old covenant and yet reformed and constituted from among all men on a spiritual basis. This instruction was to enable them to refute the attacks of the non-Christian Jews and to present to them also Jesus as their true King.[10]

1. Leon Morris, *The Gospel According to Saint Luke* (Grand Rapids, Mich.: William B. Eerdmans Publishing Company, 1974), p. 30.
2. D. Edmond Hiebert, *An Introduction to the New Testament: Volume One, the Gospels and Acts* (Chicago: Moody Press, 1975), p. 25.
3. Hiebert, p. 44.
4. J. Sidlow Baxter, *Explore the Book*, volume 5 (Grand Rapids, Mich.: Zondervan Corporation, 1966), pp. 117-125, 229.
5. Donald Guthrie, *New Testament Introduction* (Downers Grove, Ill.: InterVarsity, 1970), p. 33.
6. Hiebert, p. 49.
7. Guthrie, p. 44.
8. Hiebert., p. 66.
9. Hiebert, p. 66; Guthrie, p. 46; D. A. Carson, *The Expositor's Bible Commentary*, Volume 8 (Grand Rapids: Zondervan Publishing House, 1984), p. 21; R. A. Nixon, *The New Bible Commentary: Revised* (Grand Rapids, Mich.: Eerdmans, 1970), p. 815.
10. *The New Bible Commentary: Revised*, p. 816.

Outline of the Gospel of Matthew

A. Birth and Infancy (1:1–2:23)
    1. Genealogy of Jesus (1:1-17)
    2. The Birth of Jesus (1:18-25)
    3. The Visit of the Magi (2:1-12)
    4. Escape to Egypt (2:13-18)
    5. Return to Nazareth (2:19-23)
B. Preparation for Ministry (3:1–4:25)
    1. John the Baptist (3:1-12)
    2. The Baptism of Jesus (3:13-17)
    3. The Temptation of Jesus (4:1-11)

G. Parables of the Kingdom (13:1-52)
   1. Parable of the Sower (13:1-23)
   2. Parable of the Weeds (13:24-30)
   3. Parables of the Mustard Seed and the Yeast (13:31-35)
   4. Parable of the Weeds Explained (13:36-43)
   5. Parables of the Treasure and the Pearl (13:44-46)
   6. Parable of the Net (13:47-52)
H. The Christ Rejected (13:53–16:12)
   1. A Prophet Without Honor (13:53-58)
   2. John the Baptist is Beheaded (14:1-12)
   3. Jesus Feeds the Five Thousand (14:13-21)
   4. Jesus Walks on Water (14:22-36)
   5. Clean and Unclean (15:1-20)
   6. The Faith of the Canaanite Woman (15:21-28)
   7. The Feeding of the Four Thousand (15:29-39)
   8. The Demand for a Sign (16:1-4)
   9. The Yeast of the Pharisees and Sadducees (16:5-12)
I. Life in the Coming Kingdom (16:13–18:35)
   1. Peter's Confession of Faith (16:13-20)
   2. Jesus Predicts His Death (16:21-28)
   3. The Transfiguration (17:1-13)
   4. A Demonized Boy is Healed (17:14-23)
   5. Paying the Temple Tax (17:24-27)
   6. The Greatest in the Kingdom (18:1-9)
   7. Parable of the Lost Sheep (18:10-14)
   8. When a Brother Sins Against You (18:15-20)
   9. Parable of the Unmerciful Servant (18:21-35)
J. The Journey to Jerusalem (19:1–22:46)
   1. Jesus on Divorce (19:1-12)
   2. Jesus and Little Children (19:13-15)
   3. The Rich Young Man (19:16-30)
   4. Parable of the Vineyard (20:1-16)
   5. Jesus Predicts His Death (20:17-19)
   6. A Mother's Request (20:20-28)
   7. Blind Men Receive Their Sight (20:29-34)
   8. The Triumphal Entry (21:1-11)
   9. Jesus at the Temple (21:12-17)
   10. The Fig Tree Withers (21:18-22)
   11. Jesus' Authority Questioned (21:23-27)
   12. Parable of the Two Sons (21:28-32)
   13. Parable of the Tenants (21:33-46)
   14. Parable of the Wedding Banquet (22:1-14)
   15. Who Should Pay Tax to Caesar? (22:15-22)
   16. Marriage at the Resurrection (22:23-33)
   17. Which is the Greatest Commandment? (22:34-40)
   18. Whose Son is the Christ? (22:41-46)

K. Warnings of Judgment (23:1–25:46)
   1. Seven Woes (23:1-39)
   2. The End of the Age (24:1-35)
   3. The Day and Hour Unknown (24:36-51)
   4. Parable of the Ten Virgins (25:1-13)
   5. Parable of the Talents (25:14-30)
   6. Separating Sheep from Goats (25:31-46)
L. Jesus' Arrest, Passion, and Death (26:1–27:66)
   1. The Plot Against Jesus (26:1-5)
   2. Jesus is Anointed (26:6-13)
   3. The Betrayal Arranged (26:14-16)
   4. The Lord's Supper (26:17-30)
   5. Jesus Predicts Peter's Denial (26:31-35)
   6. The Garden of Gethsemane (26:36-46)
   7. Jesus is Arrested (26:47-56)
   8. Jesus before the Sanhedrin (26:57-68)
   9. Peter Disowns Jesus (26:69-75)
   10. Judas Hangs Himself (27:1-10)
   11. Jesus before Pilate (27:11-26)
   12. Soldiers Mock Jesus (27:27-31)
   13. The Crucifixion (27:32-44)
   14. The Death of Jesus (27:45-56)
   15. The Burial of Jesus (27:57-61)
   16. The Tomb Guarded (27:62-66)
M. Resurrection (28:1-20)
   1. The Resurrection of Jesus (28:1-10)
   2. The Report of the Guards (28:11-15)
   3. The Great Commission (28:16-20)

Map of Palestine in Jesus' time

Sidon

Tyre

Caesarea Philippi

GALILEE

Bethsadia

Capernaum
Gennesaret

Sea of Galilee

MEDITERRANEAN SEA

Nazareth

DECAPOLIS

Gerasa

River

Jordan

Jericho

Jerusalem

JUDEA

Matthew 1:1–2:23

Overview, Birth, and Infancy

The best way to introduce yourself to Matthew's Gospel is to read it through, in one sitting if possible. It should take you a little under two hours if you read quickly for an overall impression. If your Bible includes subtitles for passages, use them as clues to the story's movement.

As you read, jot down answers to questions 1-6. Questions 7-16 relate to the beginning of Matthew's Gospel.

First impressions

1. a. Read through Matthew quickly. After your first reading, what are your first impressions of Matthew's book?

_____

_____

_____

_____

_____

   b. What overall impression does it give you of Jesus?

_____

As you work your way through Matthew, note the Gospel's many quotations of Old Testament passages. Which books are most frequently quoted? What significance do you see in the pattern?

_____

_____

_____

_____

c. If you had to pick a single term to describe this Gospel, what would it be?

_____

_____

_____

_____

2. Repetition is a clue to the ideas an author wants to stress. What key words or phrases does Matthew (or Jesus) use over and over?

_____

_____

_____

_____

_____

_____

3. Look for at least one example of each of the following words or phrases found throughout Matthew's Gospel:

Fulfill _____

_____

_____

John the Baptist _____

_____

_____

The kingdom of heaven _____

_____

The healing of the sick _____

_____

Parables _____

_____

Gentiles _____

_____

Future events _____

_____

The Son of David _____

_____

Pharisees and Sadducees _____

_____

4. The practice of outlining helps us get a good grasp of the flow and general contents of a book. Fill in the following broad outline. A detailed outline (different from the one below) appears on pages 14–17.

1:1–2:23   The Person of the King

_____

_____

_____

_____

3:1–4:16   The Preparation of the King

_____

_____

_____

4:17–9:34   The Precepts of the King

_____

_____

_____

9:35–16:20   The Program of the King

_____

_____

_____

16:21–27:66   The Passion of the King

_____

_____

_____

28:1-20   The Power of the King

_____

_____

_____

_____

5. Note here any incidents, teachings, topics, or impressions of Jesus in Matthew's Gospel that you want to think about this week.

_____

_____

_____

_____

_____

6. In your first reading of Matthew's Gospel or in the background on pages 11-18, you may have encountered some concepts you'd like clarified or questions you'd like answered. While your thoughts are still fresh, jot down your questions here. You can look for answers as you study further.

_____

_____

_____

_____

_____

Jesus' genealogy and birth (1:1-25)

Genealogy (1:1). Genealogies in the Ancient Near East were used not only to show family relationships, but also economic, tribal, and political ones. Frequently they included only the most important members in the line, thus skipping over several links in the chain. Matthew does this, for example, in moving from Boaz to David, listing only two generations between them, when in fact several generations had come and gone. This is not an error; Matthew did this deliberately. Perhaps because the numerical equivalent of David's name is fourteen in Hebrew (and Jesus is the "Son of David"), Matthew lists fourteen generations between Abraham and David, David and the exile, and the exile and Jesus.[1]

7. a. What names do you recognize in the genealogy of 1:1-17?

_____

_____

_____

_____

b. Which names in the list are unfamiliar to you?

_____

_____

_____

_____

c. What do you think Matthew hoped to accomplish by beginning his Gospel with a genealogy?

_____

_____

_____

_____

_____

_____

8. a. Of the four women Matthew lists in his geneal-ogy, the first three were Gentiles, and the last was

married to a Gentile before he was killed. Why do
you think Matthew makes special mention of
these women?

_____

_____

_____

b. What is he trying to convey to his readers?

_____

_____

_____

***Expose her to public disgrace . . . divorce her qui-
etly*** (1:19). "Joseph . . . could not in conscience
marry Mary who was now thought to be unfaith-
ful. And because such a marriage would have been
a tacit admission of his own guilt, and also
because he was unwilling to expose her to the disgrace of public divorce, Joseph therefore chose a
quieter way, permitted by the law itself."[2]

From the Holy Spirit (1:20). The conception of Jesus
was a result of the direct activity of God the Holy
Spirit.

The name Jesus (1:21). "Jesus" is the Greek form of
"Joshua," which in Hebrew means either "Yahweh
is salvation" or "Yahweh saves."

---

9. Why is 1:22-23 so crucial to Matthew's account of
Jesus' birth?

_____

_____

_____

_____

_____

For Thought and Discussion: Compare Matthew's version of Jesus' birth in 1:18-25 with Luke's version in Luke 1:26–2:20. How are they similar? What differs between them?

10. a. Controversy has always surrounded the story of "the virgin birth." How does Matthew explain the virgin birth?

_____

_____

_____

_____

_____

b. Why is the virgin birth so important to Matthew's Gospel?

_____

_____

_____

_____

The visit of the Magi (2:1-12)

King Herod (2:1). Often called "Herod the Great," he ruled from 37–4 B.C. He was ruthless in both consolidating and keeping power, even executing his wife Mariamne in 29 B.C., his mother-in-law Alexandra in 28 B.C., and his brother-in-law Costobarus in 25 B.C. He was married ten times and changed his will six times to try to satisfy the desires of each of his wives regarding royal succession.[3]

Magi from the east (2:1). Most likely astrologers, perhaps from Persia or southern Arabia, both of which lie east of Israel.[4]

His star (2:2). The nature of this "star" has been debated for centuries. There are several possibilities: (1) a conjunction of planets, some with messianic significance in ancient astrology; (2) a supernova; (3) a comet; (4) a supernatural occurrence. There is no way definitively to answer the question. Yet its purpose is crystal clear: the "star," whatever it was, heralded the birth of Jesus, the Messiah. Some scholars believe Matthew uses language deliberately alluding to Numbers 24:17, "A star will come out of Jacob; a scepter will rise out of Israel."

Bethlehem in Judea (2:5). The town where David was born and reared; also the place near where Jacob buried Rachel (Genesis 35:19) and where Ruth met Boaz (Ruth 1:22–2:6).

Gifts of gold . . . incense . . . myrrh (2:11). The "incense" was a "glittering, odorous gum obtained by making incisions in the bark of several trees; myrrh exudes from a tree found in Arabia and a few other places and was a much-valued spice and perfume used in embalming."[5]

11. a. Why did the Magi go to Jerusalem?

_____

_____

_____

_____

b. How did Herod react to their visit? Why?

_____

_____

_____

_____

12. a. Why did Herod call the Magi "secretly" (2:7)?

_____

_____

_____

_____

Optional Application:
When was the last time
you spontaneously "fell
down and worshiped
him" and "presented
him with precious gifts"?
Take some time this
week—outside of a for-
mal church service—to
worship your King in this
way.

b. What information did he want from them?

_____

_____

_____

c. How did he intend to use the information they
had (see 2:16)?

_____

_____

_____

13. a. How did the Magi react when they found Jesus?

_____

_____

_____

b. Do their actions provide any kind of example for
us? Explain.

_____

_____

_____

_____

Egypt and Nazareth (2:13-23)

Two years old and under (2:16). Herod knew from
the information given him by the Magi that the
boy Jesus must be between six and twenty months
old at this time; hence the order to kill all boys two
years old and under was intended to eradicate any
possible threat to his throne.

Herod died (2:19). Traditionally thought to have
occurred in 4 B.C.

28

14. a. If Jesus was truly God's Son and the chosen Messiah, why would God instruct His Son's family to flee to Egypt rather than confront the enemy?

_____

_____

_____

_____

  b. What does this early incident teach us about what was to come?

_____

_____

_____

_____

Study Skill—Themes and Purposes
Before you study a book in detail, it is helpful to make some tentative conclusions about the book's themes and purposes. A *theme* is a main topic that recurs through the book, such as "the Messiah." A *purpose* is a reason the author wrote, such as "to teach Jewish readers that Jesus is the Messiah."
    One reading of Matthew's Gospel may not give you a firm sense of his main themes and purposes, but by now you probably are at least beginning to have some ideas about what they may be. Don't be hesitant to express those ideas; remember, they're tentative!

Archelaus (2:22). The son of Herod the Great and Malthace (Herod's fourth wife). He ruled over Judea and Samaria for ten years, 4 B.C. to A.D. 6.

Galilee (2:22). A region north of Jerusalem. After Herod the Great's death, it was governed by Herod Antipas who was given the title *tetrarch.*

Nazareth (2:23). An obscure town not mentioned in the Old Testament. It served as Jesus' hometown.

For Thought and Discussion: How do you normally react when you encounter a "Bible difficulty" such as the one in 2:23? How do your unbelieving friends react? How do you respond?

Your response

15. a. Dreams occur frequently in Matthew 1–2 as a means of divine guidance (see 1:20; 2:12,13,19,22). Why do you think Matthew highlights these incidents?

_____

_____

_____

b. Note that the only other such incident in this Gospel is recorded in 27:19, and in no case were the people involved looking for such guidance. Is this significant? If so, how?

_____

_____

_____

"He shall be called a Nazarene"

Matthew 2:23 seems to be a quotation from the Old Testament: "He will be called a Nazarene." Yet no such reference in the Old Testament exists.

Scholars have puzzled over this problem for centuries. Today most scholars would probably agree that Matthew's words "probably refer to several Old Testament . . . predictions that the Messiah would be despised (e.g., Ps. 22:6; Isa. 53:3), for in Jesus' day 'Nazarene' was virtually a synonym for 'despised' (see Jn. 1:45-46). Some hold that in speaking of Jesus as a 'Nazarene,' Matthew is referring primarily to the word 'Branch' (Hebrew neser) in Isa. 11:1."[6]

---

16. From what you know of Matthew's Gospel so far, summarize in your own words what you think is the purpose of this book.

_____

_____

_____

_____

_____

_____

_____

An ordinary outline of Matthew's Gospel such as the one on pages 14–17 can help you find particular passages, but it tells you little of how the parts fit into Matthew's overall message. One way to recall Matthew's message at a glance is to outline the way each passage unfolds that purpose.

For instance, one of Matthew's purposes is to show that Jesus is the Son of David foretold in the Old Testament. A broad outline of the book that takes account of this purpose might begin like this:

1:1–17	Genealogy: Matthew creates a bridge between the Old Testament and his book by showing that Jesus is a direct descendant of both David and Abraham.
1:18–2:23	Infancy: The Savior is born miraculously into our world, announced by angels and prophets, worshiped by Gentile rulers, and preserved by divine intervention. The King of Israel has arrived.
3:1–4:11	Preparation: The Savior's herald introduces the good news about repentance and forgiveness. The Savior is declared Son of God and undergoes baptism and temptation—all in preparation to begin His mission.

Get a sheet of paper and begin your own outline of Matthew's Gospel that reflects his purpose and themes. You can make up your own summaries for 1:1–4:11 or copy these and begin your own outline with 4:12-17. Try to add a new entry as you complete each lesson.

17. a. What issues in your own life have been raised by your quick reading of Matthew?

_____

_____

_____

_____

b. How will you deal with these issues in the coming week?

_____

_____

_____

_____

Study Skill — Summarizing the Passage
A good way to see whether you have understood a passage of Scripture is to try summarizing it in your own words. When the passage tells a story like Matthew 1:18–2:23, it can be helpful to write not just what happened, but also what the events have to do with the main themes and purposes of the book.

For the group

Warm-up. The genealogy of Jesus is crucial to Matthew's purpose in writing his Gospel. Begin this lesson by having group members share something unique or interesting from their own family trees. This will help members get to know each other and begin the discussion of Jesus' genealogy.

Discussion. As you share your responses from this lesson, compare your answers with each other. Be sure to pay special attention to questions 4, 6, and 13 as you discuss your answers. Remember, you're not looking for a "right" answer, since many of these questions ask for your opinion. Sharing answers helps give insight into the passage and often will enlighten a troublesome point.

Wrap-up. Close by thanking God for bringing your group together and for the different strengths you each bring. Thank God too for the gift of His Son and the humble way in which He came to earth.

1. D. A. Carson, "Matthew" in *The Expositor's Bible Commentary: Volume 8* (Grand Rapids, Mich.: Zondervan Publishing House, 1984), p. 62; R. E. Nixon, "Matthew" in *The New Bible Commentary: Revised* (Grand Rapids, Mich.: Eerdmans Publishing Co., 1970), p. 818.
2. Carson, p. 75.
3. "Herodian Dynasty" in *The Oxford Companion to the Bible*, eds. Bruce M. Metzger and Michael D. Coogan (New York: Oxford University Press, 1993), p. 282.
4. *The NIV Study Bible* (Grand Rapids, Mich.: Zondervan Bible Publishers, 1985), p. 1442.
5. Carson, p. 89.
6. *The NIV Study Bible*, p. 1444.

Matthew 3:1–4:25

Baptism and Temptation

Many years have passed between Matthew 2 and 3. At the end of chapter 2, Jesus was a boy; by chapter 3, He is a young man about to begin His ministry. But before He begins that ministry, two important events must take place.

The initial twelve verses of Matthew 3 describe the ministry of John the Baptist, sent to "prepare the way" for the coming Messiah. John baptizes the Christ, inaugurating his own ministry. Immediately following that, another "baptism" occurs, a baptism of fire where Jesus faces terrible temptation. By successfully overcoming this temptation, the Messiah proves ready to undertake His Father's work.

Before answering the following questions, carefully read Matthew 3 and 4, preferably in several translations. Notice especially how Matthew tells the story to convince his readers that Jesus is the promised Messiah.

John prepares the way (3:1-12)

John the Baptist (3:1). The forerunner and relative of Jesus, born to the priest Zechariah and his wife Elizabeth in about 7 B.C. Luke 1:5-25,39-45 gives more background on John's early connections to Jesus.

Camel's hair ... leather belt ... locusts and wild honey (3:4). Clothes of camel's hair and a leather

For Thought and Discussion: How do you think people would respond to John today if he came preaching the same message? Explain.

belt not only showed John was poor, but connected him with the austere lifestyles of former prophets such as Elijah. Locusts are still eaten today and are listed among the "clean" foods of Numbers. Both his clothes and food suggest that John knew a great deal about wilderness living.

Pharisees (3:7). A legalistic party of Jews who separated themselves from those who did not join in their practices. They strictly, but often hypocritically, kept the law of Moses as well as the "tradition of the elders" (see Matthew 15:2).

Sadducees (3:7). A much smaller group than the Pharisees, more worldly and politically minded. They denied such doctrines as the resurrection, angels, and spirits.

1. a. What message did John preach?

_____

_____

_____

b. How did the people respond?

_____

_____

_____

_____

2. How does Isaiah describe John's ministry (3:3)?

_____

_____

_____

_____

_____

36

3. a. Why do you think John reacted to the Pharisees and Sadducees in the way that he did (3:7-10)?

_____

_____

_____

_____

b. What prompted such a reaction?

_____

_____

_____

_____

For Further Study: John told the religious leaders of his day to "produce fruit in keeping with repentance" (3:8). Compare this with Matthew 12:33-35, Acts 26:20, Titus 1:16. What do these passages have in common?

4. a. What warning does John give in 3:10?

_____

_____

_____

b. Who was he warning?

_____

_____

_____

5. What characteristics does John use to describe the one coming after him (3:11-12)? List the characteristics he mentions, and explain why each is significant.

characteristic	significance

The baptism of Jesus (3:13-17)

"Fulfill all righteousness" (3:15). The baptism of Jesus showed that He was consecrated to God.

Heaven was opened (3:16). Reminiscent of several Old Testament passages where "visions" of heaven were given. (See Isaiah 6:1, Ezekiel 1:1.)

6. Jesus came from Galilee to the Jordan specifically to be baptized by John (3:13). Why do you think Jesus did this, especially since John's baptism was one of repentance?

_____

_____

_____

_____

_____

7. Why did John try to deter Jesus from being baptized (3:14)?

_____

_____

38

_____

_____

8. a. What was "proper" about Jesus being baptized by John (3:15)?

_____

_____

_____

_____

_____

b. How did it "fulfill all righteousness"?

_____

_____

_____

_____

_____

9. What is significant about each of the things that happened after Jesus' baptism?

Heaven opened_____

_____

_____

Spirit of God descending like a dove_____

_____

_____

Voice from heaven _____

_____

_____

Optional Application: If you have not yet been baptized, consider making arrangements to do so. For more about baptism, study the following texts: Acts 2:38-41, 8:26-39; Romans 6:3-4; 1 Peter 3:21-22.

For Thought and Discussion: If heaven opened and God were to say something about you, what do you think it would be? Why?

For Further Study:
In the Temptation
encounter in the desert,
both Jesus and Satan
quoted Scripture. What
can you learn from
Jesus' use of Scripture?
From Satan's use of
Scripture?

The Temptation of Jesus (4:1-11)

Fasting forty days and forty nights (4:2). Probably total abstention from food, but not from drink. Note several parallels with Israel's wilderness wanderings: Jesus fasted for forty days and Israel wandered for forty years; both spent time in the desert to prepare them for a future mission and both were tested by God.

10. Jesus was "led" into the desert by the Spirit specifically to be "tempted by the devil" (4:1). Why do you think the Spirit would lead Jesus into such a difficult situation?

_____

_____

_____

_____

_____

11. a. List the three temptations Matthew describes and Jesus' response to each of them:

temptation	response

b. What can we learn from Jesus about how we should respond to temptation?

_____

_____

40

_____

_____

12. a. What is Jesus' final response to Satan's temptations (4:10)?

_____

_____

_____

b. How does Satan react?

_____

_____

c. What does this show about the authority of Jesus?

_____

_____

_____

13. a. Why is 4:11 important to this incident?

_____

_____

_____

_____

b. What does it tell us about Jesus?

_____

_____

_____

_____

_____

Jesus begins to preach (4:12-17)

John had been put in prison (4:12). Matthew 14:3-4
   gives the reason for John's imprisonment. This
   event was probably not the reason for Jesus'
   return, but coincided with Jesus' plans.

Capernaum (4:13). Apparently a large town. Peter
   owned a house there that became the disciples'
   base of operations while in Galilee (Mark 2:1,
   9:33).

14. Matthew connects Jesus' move from Nazareth to
   Capernaum with a prophecy from Isaiah 9:1-2.
   What does he want his readers to see?

_____

_____

_____

_____

15. a. Note that Jesus' message in 4:17 is identical to
   John's in 3:2. How is this significant?

_____

_____

_____

_____

42

b. What is Matthew trying to show?

_____

_____

_____

_____

_____

_____

Jesus calls the first disciples (4:18-25)

16. a. How did Jesus call the first disciples (4:19)?

_____

_____

_____

b. How did they respond?

_____

_____

_____

_____

43

The good news of the kingdom (4:23). "The term recurs in 9:35, 24:14, and becomes 'this gospel' in 26:13. . . . The 'good news' concerns the kingdom, whose 'nearness' has already been announced and which is the central subject of the Sermon on the Mount."[1]

The Decapolis (4:25). Literally, the ten cities. They were "a league of free cities characterized by high Greek culture. All but one, Scythopolis (Beth Shan), were east of the Sea of Galilee and the Jordan [River]."[2] The league stretched from a point northeast of the Sea of Galilee southward to Philadelphia (modern Amman).

17. What three things was Jesus doing throughout Galilee(4:23)?

_____

_____

_____

_____

_____

18. a. How did the people respond to Jesus' ministry (4:24-25)?

_____

_____

_____

_____

b. Had you been living in Israel at that time, how do you think you would have responded? Explain.

_____

_____

_____

_____

44

Your response

19. a. What one insight from this lesson would you like to focus on for application this week?

_____

_____

_____

b. Write down at least one way in which this insight is relevant to your actions toward God, other people, or circumstances.

_____

_____

_____

c. What concrete steps can you take (consistent prayer, a decision, a change of attitude toward circumstances, action, etc.) in light of this insight?

_____

_____

_____

For the group

Warm-up. Begin this lesson by sharing a time when you were facing a major life transition (marriage, job change, first job, etc.). What did you do to prepare yourself for that change?

Discussion. As you work through this lesson, keep an eye open for ways to apply what you learn. The study skill on application may help as you do this. Often, a particular application comes from another person, which is one of the reasons why group Bible study is so beneficial.

Prayer. As Christians, we often face temptation to stray from God and His truth. Share with each other how you have faced temptation in the past, and how Jesus' example in this lesson will help you face temptation in the future. Encourage each other to use Scripture in situations where temptation exists and pray that God will strengthen your resistance to Satan's attacks.

1. D. A. Carson, "Matthew" in *The Expositor's Bible Commentary: Volume 8* (Grand Rapids:, Mich.: Zondervan Publishing House, 1984), p. 121.
2. *The NIV Study Bible* (Grand Rapids, Mich.: Zondervan Bible Publishers, 1985), p. 1449.

Matthew 5:1–7:29

The Sermon on the Mount

Without question, the Sermon on the Mount is the most-studied, best-known sermon in history. It has been dissected, analyzed, inspected, discussed, and pondered in countless ways by untold numbers of students throughout the centuries, yet its message continues both to challenge and confound readers today.

What gives the sermon its power? Why has it continued to hold such a central place in the study of the Gospels? How are we to understand it—and more to the point, obey it? What does Jesus want to teach us in this sermon, and how are we to respond to His lesson?

As you read through Matthew 5:1–7:29, look especially for two strands of teaching that often have confused readers through the ages: God's perfect and holy standards and His great grace offered to unworthy sinners. As you note both strands, see how Jesus presented both truths so that we might be able to come into a right relationship with His Father.

The Beatitudes (5:1-12)

He went up on a mountainside (5:1). Not a "mountain" as we generally think of it, but perhaps a gently sloping hillside at the northwest corner of the Sea of Galilee.[1]

47

Blessed (5:3). "The word means more than 'happy,' because happiness is an emotion often dependent on outward circumstances. 'Blessed' here refers to the ultimate well-being and distinctive spiritual joy of those who share in the salvation of the kingdom of God."[2]

Poor in spirit (5:3). As opposed to the spiritually proud and self-sufficient.

Meek (5:5). The attitude of humility, especially in the presence of God.

Pure in heart (5:8). Some commentators believe this phrase refers to inner moral purity (contrasted with merely external piety or ceremonial cleanness); others believe it refers to singlemindedness, the "utterly sincere." Either way, this beatitude condemns hypocrisy.

---

1. a. The portion of Scripture we call the Beatitudes (5:1-12) is one of the most familiar passages in the Bible, and often one of the least pondered. To gain a new appreciation for it, try "reversing" the Beatitudes. Rephrase them from an inverse point of view (for example, "Miserable are the arrogant, for theirs is the kingdom of hell.").

_____

_____

_____

_____

_____

_____

_____

_____

_____

b. Did you learn anything new from the Beatitudes when studied this way? If so, what?

_____

_____

_____

_____

_____

For Further Study:
Compare the Beatitudes with the teaching Jesus gave "on a level place" as recorded in Luke 6:17-26. How are these teachings similar?

2. a. "Blessed are those who are persecuted because of righteousness . . ." is the only Beatitude that receives further comment. How does 5:11-12 expand on it?

_____

_____

_____

_____

b. Why do you think this Beatitude alone was singled out for expanded treatment?

_____

_____

_____

_____

Salt and light (5:13-16)

Salt (5:13). In the ancient world, salt was used to flavor foods, to fertilize, but primarily to preserve foods. When a little salt was rubbed into meat, it would slow the decaying process.

Optional Application:
How are you "salt" and
"light" in your commu-
nity? List any areas in
which your "salt" may
have lost its savor or
your "light" may be hid-
den. What can you do
today to change?

3. a. Jesus says that we are salt and light. How are we
like salt and light?

Salt _____

_____

_____

Light _____

_____

_____

b. What happens when salt and light are not used
as intended?

_____

_____

_____

The fulfillment of the law (5:17-20)

But I tell you (5:18). In the Old Testament, the
prophets had always said, "Thus says the
Lord . . . ." Jesus did not do that; He put the
emphasis on Himself, "I tell you . . . ."

4. a. How did Jesus "fulfill" the law (5:17-20)?

_____

_____

_____

_____

b. What does it mean to "fulfill" the law, and why is
this important?

_____

_____

50

_____

_____

_____

Murder, adultery, and divorce (5:21-32)

5. Imagine you are in the crowd Jesus is addressing. Why might His words on murder shock you (5:21-24)?

_____

_____

_____

_____

_____

6. a. How might people misunderstand Jesus' main point in 5:27-30?

_____

_____

_____

b. Far from abolishing the law, what does Jesus do here?

_____

_____

_____

For Thought and Discussion: Divorce is rampant in our society and almost as common in the church. How should the church respond to divorce, both in principle and in practice? Should divorced persons be restricted at all in ministry opportunities through the church? Explain.

For Further Study: Look up the following texts and discuss what bearing they have on the issue of divorce: Matthew 19:1-12; Mark 10:1-12; Luke 16:18; John 4:1-26; 1 Corinthians 7:10-16,39-40.

For Further Study: There is a difference between an "oath" and a "vow." While both are solemn promises, an "oath" calls upon God or some other revered person or thing to witness the promise. See Deuteronomy 23:21-23; Psalm 76:11; Proverbs 20:25; Acts 18:18; 23:12,14,21; James 5:12.

> **Study Skill—Hyperbole**
> Hyperbole is extreme exaggeration to make a point; it was a common Hebrew form of expression. In Matthew 5:29-30, Jesus doesn't mean that we should literally pluck out our right eye and cut off our right hand as a means to overcoming lust—He understands perfectly well that if we actually did such a thing, we'd still have a left eye and a left hand we could use to continue lusting. His point is that lust is as grievous a sin to God as actual adultery. Jesus wants us to see that God's standards are much higher than we can ever realize, and that our only hope is in Him.

Oaths, eyes, and enemies (5:33-48)

7. a. What is the problem with giving oaths, according to 5:33-37?

_____

_____

_____

_____

b. What should we do instead? Why?

_____

_____

_____

_____

8. Are Jesus' words in 5:38-42 a call to renounce self-defense? Why or why not?

_____

_____

_____

_____

_____

9. How is it possible to love your enemies (5:43-47)?

_____

_____

_____

_____

Optional Application:
Who are your "ene-
mies"? Focus on the
person who could be
considered your "chief
enemy" and, this week,
reach out to him or her
with some practical show
of love.

10. a. Sometimes people try to soften the command-
    ment of 5:48 by insisting that it tells us to be
    "mature" rather than "perfect." Yet the same
    Greek word (*teleios*) is used both of us and God.
    What would be wrong in using the term
    "mature" to translate the word *teleios* here?

_____

_____

_____

_____

  b. What is Jesus wanting us to see here?

_____

_____

_____

_____

Giving to the needy (6:1-4)

11. a. How are we to do acts of charity, according to
    6:1-3?

_____

_____

_____

_____

_____

Optional Application:
Is there someone you
need to forgive in order
to receive God's
forgiveness?

b. Why do you think we so often violate this
command?

_____

_____

_____

Prayer and fasting (6:5-18)

12. How does Jesus tell us to pray (6:5-8)?

_____

_____

_____

_____

13. How is forgiveness connected to our praying? Why?

_____

_____

_____

_____

14. a. How is Jesus' teaching on fasting (6:16-18) similar to His teaching on prayer (6:5-15)?

_____

_____

_____

b. Why are things done in secret so important to
God?

_____

_____

_____

_____

Treasures and worries (6:19-34)

15. a. Why is it impossible to serve two masters?

_____

_____

_____

b. How does this teaching connect with the Lord's teaching on "treasures on earth"?

_____

_____

_____

16. What reasons does Jesus give for refusing to worry (6:25-34)?

_____

_____

_____

_____

"Do not judge" (7:1-6)

17. How does 7:3-5 help define the kind of "judging" Jesus is talking about in 7:1-2?

_____

_____

_____

Optional Application: Fasting in the Bible usually means going without all food and drink for a period in order to concentrate on spiritual matters. Choose a day this week and try fasting. Note in a journal what you were feeling and thinking, and especially how the Lord used the fast to concentrate your energies on some spiritual goal.

For Thought and Discussion: What do you worry about? Share with the group and discuss how to apply Jesus' instruction not to worry.

55

For Thought and Discussion: If the nature of evangelism is to present the gospel to unbelievers, how can believers avoid giving "dogs" what is sacred or throwing their "pearls" to "pigs"? How does one discern "dogs" and "pigs" from those who may be open to the gospel?

Study Skill—Context

It is crucial to read individual commands in light of the whole passage, the entire book, and the rest of Scripture. The command, "Do not judge" (Matthew 7:1) is a good example. Elsewhere, Jesus commands us to discern right from wrong in ourselves and others (Matthew 7:15-20; Luke 6:43-45, 7:43, 12:57; compare Acts 4:19). Therefore, we must understand the word "judge" in light of Matthew 7:1-5.

Here, to judge is to pass judgment on the motivations of someone's heart, to declare what he justly deserves, and furthermore to wish heartily that he will get everything that is coming to him. Jesus warns us against judging the intentions or motivations of someone's heart—that is something known to God alone. Since we cannot know what is in someone's heart, we are to "judge nothing before the appointed time" when the Lord will "bring to light what is hidden in darkness and will expose the motives of men's hearts" (1 Corinthians 4:5).

Dogs . . . pigs (7:6). A picture of what is wild, unclean, vicious and abominable. Dogs were not generally household pets in New Testament times, but were despised scavengers.

18. How does Jesus' advice about dogs and pigs fit with 5:38-42?

_____

_____

_____

_____

Ask, seek, knock (7:7-12)

19. Is the picture of God in verses 7-11 how you normally think of Him? Explain.

_____

_____

56

_____

_____

_____

The narrow and wide gates (7:13-14)

20. a. What does this passage teach about the way of salvation?

_____

_____

_____

b. Would you call this inclusive or exclusive? Why?

_____

_____

_____

_____

Trees and fruit (7:15-23)

21. a. What does Jesus mean by "fruit"?

_____

_____

b. What kind of "fruit" are you bearing?

_____

_____

For Further Study: Our society tends to frown on ideas or doctrines that seem "narrow" or "exclusive." Yet the Bible is clear that Jesus is the only way to heaven. See the following texts: John 14:6, Acts 4:8-12, Romans 10:5-13, 1 Corinthians 15:13-18, 1 Timothy 2:5.

For Further Study: The Bible has a great deal to say about "false prophets." Consider the following passages: Jeremiah 14:13-16, 23:9-40; Ezekiel 13; Matthew 24:11,24; Acts 13:6, 20:29-31; 2 Corinthians 11:13; 2 Peter 2:1-3; 1 John 4:1-3.

For Further Study:
The Bible places much
emphasis on the idea of
"fruit" in a believer's life.
Note the following pas-
sages: Matthew 12:33,
John 15:1-16, Romans
7:4, Galatians 5:22,
Ephesians 5:9, Philip-
pians 1:11, Colossians
1:10, James 3:17.

Wise and foolish builders (7:24-29)

22. How does 7:24-27 summarize Jesus' teaching on the Sermon on the Mount?

_____

_____

_____

_____

_____

_____

23. According to 7:28-29, how did the crowds react to Jesus' teaching?

_____

_____

_____

_____

_____

For the group

Warm-up. Begin this week's lesson by asking the following question, "When you were a kid, did you generally follow the rules, or did you always push the limits?"
  Our attitudes toward rules can influence the way
we read the Sermon on the Mount with its instructions
for living the Christian life and its command to "be perfect." Knowing how we approach rules will help us better understand our response to this lesson.

Discussion. As you work through this lesson, share
your favorite part of the Sermon on the Mount or a passage you noticed for the first time during this reading of
it. Why did that particular passage stand out to you?

Wrap-up. There are many areas of application found in this lesson. Jesus' teaching in the Sermon on the Mount is specific and applies directly to life today. Close this lesson by sharing one area of application you'd like to focus on this week. Pray for each other and commit to pray for one other person in the group during the upcoming week.

1. *The NIV Study Bible* (Grand Rapids, Mich.: Zondervan Bible Publishers, 1985), p. 1449.
2. *The NIV Study Bible,* p. 1449.

Matthew 8:1–9:34

Jesus at Work

After describing the crowd's response to Jesus' *teaching*—"because he taught as one who had authority, and not as their teachers of the law" (Matthew 7:29)—Matthew moves on to show that Jesus' *actions* also went beyond the ordinary and the expected.

In this lesson we see Jesus' power over leprosy, one of the most dreaded diseases of that time. Then in quick succession we see him cure people of paralysis, fevers, demon possession, long-term hemorrhages, blindness, the inability to speak—even reversing death itself.

But despite all this evidence, the local religious leaders come to an incredible conclusion: they proclaim that Jesus does all these miraculous works by the power of the devil, not by the power of God. Amazing as it may seem, not even miracles can force someone to believe. Faith cannot bloom where the will is stony, cold, and hard. Faith is not only a matter of the heart, but also of the will. As you study Matthew 8–9, look for this emphasis.

Leaving the mountain (8:1-4)

Leprosy (8:2). Not necessarily the disease we know today as leprosy (Hansen's disease), but any number of skin ailments abhorred by Jews not only for the affliction they brought, but because of the ceremonial uncleanness they caused.

61

For Further Study:
Jesus often instructed those He healed not to tell how they were cured. See Matthew 12:16; Mark 1:44, 3:12, 7:36; Luke 5:14, 8:56. Why do you think He gave such commands?

Clean (8:2). Leviticus 13-14 instructed that anyone with such a skin disease was "unclean." To be cured of the disease meant one was now "clean."

Jesus . . . touched the man (8:3). "By touching an unclean leper, Jesus would become ceremonially defiled himself. But at Jesus' touch nothing remains defiled. Far from becoming unclean, Jesus makes the unclean clean."[1]

1. Note that in 8:1-4, the man afflicted with leprosy never questioned Jesus' *ability* to heal, but rather His *willingness* to heal. Do you think people share this same doubt today? Why?

_____

_____

_____

_____

_____

2. a. Why did Jesus instruct the healed man to "show [himself] to the priest"?

_____

_____

_____

_____

  b. Why do you think Jesus instructed the man not to tell anyone what had happened?

_____

_____

_____

_____

The centurion's faith (8:5-13)

Centurion (8:8). A Roman legion had sixty centurions, men of officer rank who corresponded to company commanders. They "were men of status in the community and had a wide range of expertise and experience. Their duties often ranged beyond the strictly regimental, even to judicial functions and the administration of small military districts."[2]

3. Why didn't the centurion want Jesus to come to his house (8:7-9)?

_____

_____

_____

_____

4. How does Jesus' encounter with the centurion prompt His response in Matthew 8:11-12?

_____

_____

_____

_____

_____

For Thought and Discussion: a. Only a few times in the Gospel is Jesus said to be "astonished" or "amazed." See Matthew 8:10, Mark 6:6, and Luke 7:9. How is faith involved?

b. Similarly, Jesus complimented only two people on their faith (Matthew 8:10, 15:28). In both cases, it is a Gentile whose faith is complimented. How is this significant?

63

Optional Application:
Pick an area of life in
which you would like to
increase your faith in
God. Then brainstorm
ways to increase your
faith in that area. Pick
one, put it into practice,
and note the outcome in
a journal.

Jesus heals many (8:14-17)

Peter's mother-in-law (8:14). Peter was married (see
also 1 Corinthians 9:5) and apparently had moved
with his brother Andrew from Bethsaida (John
1:44) to Capernaum, perhaps to remain near
Jesus.

5. a. List the ailments Jesus cured in 8:14-17, along
with the methods He used.

ailment cured	method used

b. What do you learn from this?

_____

_____

_____

_____

6. Matthew 8:17 says that Jesus' healing ministry fulfilled Isaiah 53:4. What does he want his readers
to see?

_____

_____

_____

_____

Following Jesus (8:18-27)

7. a. Jesus interacts with two men in 8:18-22. What
   does each man say to Jesus and how does Jesus
   respond?

man's request	Jesus' response

b. How do each of these challenges still confront us
   today?

_____

_____

_____

_____

A furious storm (8:24). The Sea of Galilee often plays
host to sudden, violent squalls because it lies in a
basin surrounded by mountains. "Cool air from
the Mediterranean is drawn down through the
narrow mountain passes and clashes with the hot,
humid air lying over the lake."[3]

---

8. How does the story in 8:23-27 reveal both the disciples' faith and their doubt?

Faith _____

_____

_____

For Further Study:
People were constantly
surprised by what Jesus
said and did—even His
own disciples. Look up
the following: Matthew
7:28, 8:27, 9:33,
13:54, 15:31, 21:20,
22:22; Mark 15:5; John
5:28, 7:15.

Doubts _____

_____

_____

Jesus casts out demons (8:28-34)

9. What questions do the two demon-possessed men
address to Jesus (8:28-29)? How do their questions
identify Jesus?

question	what it reveals about Jesus

Region of the Gadarenes (8:28). A district controlled
by the town of Gadara, near the village of Gerasa.
On the adjacent hillside are ancient tombs.

A large herd of pigs (8:30). Galilee was home to a
large number of Gentiles. Jews ordinarily did not
raise pigs, since they were considered vile and
"unclean."

---

10. a. How did the town respond to Jesus' actions
(8:30-34)?

_____

_____

_____

b. How would you have responded?

_____

_____

_____

Jesus heals a paralytic (9:1-8)

11. a. Why did the "teachers of the law" believe Jesus was blaspheming in 9:2?

_____

_____

_____

b. On what did they base this belief (see Isaiah 43:25, 44:22; Psalm 51:4)?

_____

_____

_____

12. a. What is the obvious answer to Jesus' question in 9:5?

_____

_____

_____

b. How does Jesus connect His actions in 9:6-7 with this question?

_____

_____

_____

13. a. How did the crowd react in 9:8?

_____

_____

_____

b. Why?

_____

_____

For Thought and Discussion: Although the Gadarene townspeople understood that the lives of two men were saved (8:33), apparently they cared more about their own economic lives. Is this a battle we face as well? If so, in what way must we face it?

For Further Study: Jesus is reported to have known the thoughts of His opponents, an ability that was predicted shortly after His birth (Luke 2:35). See Matthew 12:25; Mark 2:8; Luke 6:8, 11:17. How does this enlarge your view of the Savior?

For Thought and Discussion: In Matthew 9:2, it is apparently the faith of the paralytic's friends that is commended, not of the paralytic himself. At other times, faith is not mentioned at all in connection with healing (Matthew 8:15; Mark 1:21-27, 7:31-35). What can we learn from these varying circumstances?

The calling of Matthew (9:9-13)

Tax collector's booth (9:9). A "customs and excise booth at the border between the territories of Philip and Herod Antipas."[4] Jews hated tax collectors not only for the sometimes excessive revenue they collected, but because they were seen as pawns and puppets of the hated Romans.

14. Matthew became one of the twelve disciples closest to Jesus. What does Jesus' choice of Matthew reveal about His attitude toward "tax collectors and 'sinners'" (9:9-13)?

_____

_____

_____

_____

_____

15. Jesus makes three statements in 9:12-13. What does each one mean, and how does it relate to you?

"It is not the healthy who need a doctor, but the sick."

_____

_____

_____

"I desire mercy, not sacrifice."

_____

_____

_____

_____

"I have not come to call the righteous, but sinners."

Showing Mercy

When Jesus quotes Hosea 6:6, "I desire mercy, not sacrifice," He makes it clear to the Pharisees that God "was not simply telling them that they should be more sympathetic to outcasts and less concerned about ceremonial purity, but that they were aligned with the apostates of ancient Israel in that they too preserved the shell while losing the heart of the matter."[5]

Brainstorm some practical ways your group can show mercy to the outcasts in your own area: serve meals at a local rescue mission; support a women's shelter; etc. Then commit to follow through on one of these ideas.

Questions about fasting (9:14-17)

16. a. How did Jesus reply to the question John's disciples asked Him (9:14-15)?

b. What did He mean by this reply?

69

17. Jesus uses two parables in 9:16-17 to describe His ministry. How do they relate to the question about fasting?

_____

_____

_____

_____

_____

A dead girl and a sick woman (9:18-26)

Flute players . . . noisy crowd (9:23). Musicians were hired to play in mourning ceremonies, and mourners were hired to wail and lament at funerals.

18. Two healings are described in 9:18-26, the first requiring more immediate attention than the second. Yet Jesus pauses on His way to the first in order to help the second. What does this teach you about His priorities? His timing?

_____

_____

_____

_____

_____

19. a. What examples of faith and of unbelief do you find in the two stories of 9:18-26?

Faith _____

_____

_____

70

Unbelief _____

_____

_____

b. What can you learn from each example?

_____

_____

_____

_____

Jesus heals the blind and mute (9:27-34)

Son of David (9:27). A popular Jewish title for the Messiah.

20. a. Matthew 9:27-31 tells how Jesus healed two blind men. From this account, what do we know about the beliefs of these men?

_____

_____

_____

b. What happened because of their actions and beliefs?

_____

_____

_____

21. a. How did the crowd react to the healing of a demon-possessed man(9:32-34)?

_____

_____

_____

_____

_____

b. How did the Pharisees react?

_____

_____

_____

c. How do you account for these marked differences?

_____

_____

_____

For the group

Warm-up. This lesson focuses on Jesus' actions—especially His ability to heal people. Begin this lesson by asking the following questions:

- Do you believe God still heals people?
- Have you ever witnessed a miraculous healing?
- If so, what was your response?

Discussion. Jesus stated that He desires mercy, not sacrifice. How can you (individually or as a group) show mercy to others? Pay special attention to "Showing Mercy" on page 69. As you go through this lesson, ask how Jesus showed people mercy and what you can learn from His example.

1. D. A. Carson, "Matthew" in *The Expositor's Bible Commentary: Volume 8* (Grand Rapids, Mich.: Zondervan Publishing House, 1984), p. 198.
2. "Centurion" in *The Oxford Companion to the Bible*, eds. Bruce M. Metzger and Michael D. Coogan (New York: Oxford University Press, 1993), p. 105.
3. *The NIV Study Bible* (Grand Rapids, Mich.: Zondervan Bible Publishers, 1985), p. 1501.
4. Carson, p. 223.
5. Carson, p. 225.

Matthew 9:35–10:42

The Mission of the Twelve

The disciples had seen their Master impress the crowds with compelling insights and remarkable words. They had witnessed Him bless the sick and dying with divine healing. They had watched Him do His Father's will and had noted the astonishing results.

And now it was their turn.

Jesus made it clear that He did not come to do the work of His Father alone. He was the teacher, and insisted that His students learn by doing. Therefore He would send out His twelve disciples into the surrounding countryside to see for themselves how the Father might use them to minister to the hurting and needy people of Israel.

But before they would be ready for such a challenging assignment, they needed some special instructions—which they received in Matthew 10:5-42. Interestingly, unlike Mark (Mark 6:12-13) and Luke (Luke 9:6-10), Matthew never tells us how the mission went. Instead he concentrates on the Messiah Himself, convincing his readers that Jesus is the Anointed One.

The Lord of the harvest (9:35-38)

1. List the elements of Jesus' ministry below (9:35). Why is each important?

_____

_____

For Thought and Discussion: Ezekiel 34 contrasts the "shepherds of Israel" with another "shepherd" ("my servant David") whom God would set over the nation. Do you think Matthew had this passage in the mind when he wrote Matthew 9:36? Explain.

2. What does 9:36 tell us about Jesus' motivation for ministry?

3. a. What is the "harvest" (9:37)?

b. How is it "plentiful"?

c. What kind of "workers" are needed?

4. Is the instruction Jesus gives in 9:38 still needed today? Explain.

_____

_____

Jesus sends out the twelve (10:1-10)

Lost sheep of Israel (10:6). The unregenerate among the Jewish people.

Do not take along (10:9). More likely means "do not procure," as the same word is used in Acts 1:18, 8:20, 22:28.[1]

_____

5. a. What did Jesus command the disciples to do (10:1)?

_____

_____

_____

b. How were they to do it?

_____

_____

_____

c. What was to be the outcome?

_____

_____

_____

6. a. The first instruction Jesus gives may sound exclusive to modern ears. Why did Jesus give this instruction?

_____

_____

_____

Optional Application:
Are you involved in the "harvest field" that surrounds you? Pray that God would send out workers into the harvest field. Then consider how you might be able to be part of the answer to your prayer.

For Further Study: "To the Jews first" is a common theme in Scripture. Consider the following texts: Mark 7:27; Acts 1:8, 13:46-48; Romans 1:16, 2:9-10, 3:1. Why do you think this theme is so prominent?

b. What Scripture can you think of that supports your answer?

_____

_____

_____

_____

7. How is preaching the message of the kingdom related to healing the sick, raising the dead, cleansing those with leprosy, and driving out demons (10:7-8)?

_____

_____

_____

_____

_____

8. a. What had the disciples "freely received" (10:8)?

_____

_____

_____

_____

b. How is this a picture of how the gospel is to operate in our own lives?

_____

_____

_____

_____

9. a. What were the disciples not to take on their journey (10:9-10)?

_____

_____

b. What was Jesus trying to teach the disciples?

For Further Study: A frequent theme in Scripture is found in Matthew 10:10, "for the worker is worth his keep." See also 1 Corinthians 9:14, 1 Timothy 5:17-18. What implications does this have for us today in the church?

A worthy person (10:11-16)

Worthy person (10:11). Probably does not refer to a morally upright or religious person but rather to a person eager to welcome an apostle of Jesus.

Let your peace rest on it (10:13) If it is a worthy home, stay there.

Shake the dust off your feet (10:14). A visual protest before God demonstrating the animosity shown to God's chosen servants.

10. a. Hospitality is mentioned frequently in the New Testament (Romans 12:13, 1 Peter 4:9, Hebrews 13:2, 3 John 8-10). Why is it an important virtue?

b. Would you be considered a "worthy" person? Explain.

77

_____

_____

11. Why do you think Jesus instructed His disciples to stay in one home in a town rather than moving from house to house (10:11)?

_____

_____

_____

_____

_____

12. The consequences for treating the disciples poorly are more severe than might be expected (10:14-15). Why?

_____

_____

_____

Be on your guard (10:17-23)

He who stands firm to the end will be saved
(10:22). Not active resistance so much as patient endurance (see Daniel 12:12, Mark 13:13, Romans 12:12, 1 Peter 2:20).

13. The disciples and the people they will come into contact with are compared to four animals (10:16). Who do they represent, and what is the significance of each?

Sheep _____

_____

_____

Wolves _____

_____

_____

Snakes _____

_____

_____

Doves _____

_____

_____

For Thought and Discussion: Godly men and women always have been persecuted. This was true in the Old Testament (Luke 11:47-48), the New Testament (Acts 8:1-3), and will be true in the future (2 Timothy 3:12, Revelation 6:9-11). Why do you think God allows this to happen?

14. a. What kind of persecution will the disciples face?

_____

_____

_____

b. Why does Jesus warn them about it?

_____

_____

_____

15. a. What promise does Jesus give the disciples (10:19-20)?

_____

_____

_____

b. Do you think this promise is still in effect today? Why, or why not?

_____

_____

_____

For Further Study:
Perseverance is another frequent theme in Scripture: see Romans 11:22; Colossians 1:22-23; 1 Timothy 4:16; Hebrews 3:13-14, 10:35-39; 2 John 9; Revelation 2:26; 3:5,12,21; 21:7.

Optional Application:
What active role do you play in encouraging other believers to "hold firmly till the end"? What could you do? Pick two or three such activities and put them into practice before the end of the week.

The Son of Man Comes

Matthew 10:23 "is among the most difficult [verses] in the NT canon," according to D. A. Carson.[2] The primary difficulty is identifying what is meant by the "coming" of the Son of Man. Evangelicals have opted for one of at least five views:

1. Jesus is speaking of "catching up" to His disciples after they finish this particular mission.
2. The "coming" is a reference to the public identification of Jesus as the Messiah, most likely after the Resurrection.
3. The Son of Man's coming in this passage should be linked to similar expressions elsewhere (Matthew 24:30, 25:31, 26:64).
4. It is a reference to the Second Coming.
5. The coming refers to Jesus' "coming in judgment against the Jews, culminating in the sack of Jerusalem and the destruction of the temple."[3]

Warnings (10:24-33)

Beelzebub (10:25). The Greek form of the Hebrew name Baal-Zebub ("lord of the flies," see 2 Kings 1:2), a mockery of the name Baal-Zebul ("Exalted Baal"). The name eventually came to be connected with Satan.[4]

16. a. What are the disciples not to fear (10:26-30)? Why?

_____

_____

_____

b. What are they to fear instead? Why?

_____

_____

_____

17. a. Jesus gives another kind of warning in 10:32-33. What is this warning?

_____

_____

_____

b. To whom is it directed?

_____

_____

_____

c. What is its purpose?

_____

_____

_____

For Thought and Discussion: Peter disowned Jesus three times (see Matthew 26:69-75), and yet was not only welcomed back into the fold (John 21:15-19), but became the leader of the church (Acts 1–2). What, then, is the force of Jesus' warning? How does it apply to us today?

Finding life (10:34-42)

18. a. How did Jesus bring a "sword" to earth (10:34-36)?

_____

_____

_____

b. Can we still see this principle at work today? How?

_____

_____

_____

19. a. What kind of commitment does Jesus want (10:37-39)?

_____

_____

_____

_____

b. Do you have this kind of commitment? Explain.

_____

_____

_____

A prophet's reward (10:41). A kingdom reward that is the fruit of discipleship.[5]

20. After delivering some sobering news, Jesus concludes His teaching in this passage with some real words of encouragement (10:40-42). What are they, and how are they meant to encourage Jesus' followers?

_____

_____

_____

_____

_____

_____

Your response

21. List any questions you have about anything in this lesson.

_____

_____

_____

_____

_____

_____

_____

For the group

Warm-up. Begin this lesson by completing the following statement with something other than "God" or a
family member: "I love . . ."

Discussion. Love is a word we use loosely. We love
chocolate, we love our families, we love to shop. As you
study this lesson, make a list of other things that people "love." After your list is complete, ask the following
question: Jesus says that we are not to love our family
members more than we love Him (10:37). What other
things get in our way of loving Jesus?

Wrap-up. As you end this lesson, choose one area of
application you'd like to focus on in the coming week.
Share with the group and again commit to pray for
another person throughout the week. Share any results
at next week's meeting.

1. D. A. Carson, "Matthew" in *The Expositor's Bible Commentary,*
   Volume 8 (Grand Rapids, Mich.: Zondervan Publishing House,
   1984), p. 245.
2. Carson, p, 250.
3. Carson, p. 252.
4. *The NIV Study Bible* (Grand Rapids, Mich.: Zondervan Bible Publishers, 1985), p. 1457.
5. Carson, p. 259.

Matthew 11:1–12:21

The Claims of Christ

Wherever Jesus went, He created a stir. Blind people saw; lame people walked; demons left at His command. Yet opinions varied as to who this Jesus really was. Was He the Son of God, the Messiah? Or was He just another impostor, a pretender, a fraud?

Although John the Baptist gave a strong testimony to the true identity of Jesus in Matthew 3:13-15, by Matthew 11 John is in prison and wondering whether he had made a mistake. Could the Messiah really be treated so harshly? Did that make sense?

Jesus answered John's painful questions by pointing to His recent work of healing and preaching. Then He would make a series of additional claims: He was the One through whom people could know the Father, the rest-giver, the Lord of the Sabbath, God's chosen servant, the Son of Man.

Jesus and John the Baptist (11:1-19)

1. a. Read Matthew 3:13-17. After such a strong testimony, why do you think John was having these second thoughts about Jesus' identity (11:1-3)?

_____

_____

_____

b. Can you think of any similar occurrences in your own life? If so, describe them.

_____

_____

_____

2. a. How did Jesus respond to John's doubts (11:4-6)?

_____

_____

_____

b. What was Jesus' encouragement to John and his disciples?

_____

_____

_____

_____

The Elijah who was to come (11:14). Malachi 4:5 predicts that Elijah the prophet will reappear in Israel before the "great and dreadful day of the LORD."

---

3. a. Jesus describes John the Baptist both by what John was and what he wasn't (11:7-11). List both descriptions below.

what John was	what John wasn't

b. How are these descriptions significant?

_____

_____

_____

_____

For Further Study:
Compare Malachi 4:1-6
with John's coming. See
also Luke 1:17, John
1:21, Matthew
17:10-13. How else
are Elijah and John the
Baptist connected?

4. a. How does Jesus describe this generation
(11:16-19)?

_____

_____

_____

_____

**For Thought and
Discussion:** What are
some of the misconcep-
tions our present gener-
ation has about Jesus
and His mission?

b. How does verse 17 relate to verses 18-19?

_____

_____

_____

_____

c. What point is Jesus making?

_____

_____

_____

_____

5. Jesus said that "wisdom is proved right by her
actions" (11:19). How does this apply to Jesus and
John?

_____

_____

_____

_____

Unrepentant cities (11:20-24)

Korazin . . . Bethsaida (11:21). Korazin was a city
that probably lay about two miles north of Capernaum. Bethsaida was another city on the northeast shore of the Sea of Galilee.

6. a. Where did Jesus perform most of His miracles
(11:20-24)?

_____

_____

_____

_____

b. How did the people respond to His message and
miracles?

_____

_____

_____

c. What did Jesus say about their reaction?

_____

_____

_____

7. a. What is significant about each of the ancient
cities Jesus mentions? (You may need to use the
resources listed on pages 199-201 to help answer
the question.)

Tyre_____

_____

Sidon_____

_____

Sodom _____

b. How does our own generation respond to Christ and the gospel?

_____

_____

_____

8. a. How did people in Jesus time show repentance (11:21)?

_____

_____

_____

b. What purpose did it serve?

_____

_____

c. What might serve the same kind of purpose today?

_____

_____

Optional Application:
Unbelief was not just a problem for people who lived long ago. Search your own heart and name some areas of your own unbelief.

For Further Study:
Read Genesis 13:10–19:30. What do you learn about "the cities of the plain"? What light does this background shed on Jesus' comments in Matthew 11:20-24?

Rest for the weary (11:25-30)

9. After Jesus spoke to the crowd and issued judgment on the unrepentant cities, He thanked His heavenly Father for revealing the truth about Him to little children (11:25-27). Why does God not reveal the truth to the wise and learned?

_____

_____

89

For Thought and Discussion: How is rest for our souls, hearts, and minds as great a need in our time as it was in Jesus' day? Think of areas where you need to find rest and meditate on Jesus' invitation to you.

10. a. What does Jesus promise if we accept His invitation?

_____

_____

_____

b. Who can accept the invitation?

_____

_____

Lord of the Sabbath (12:1-14)

11. a. The Pharisees were eager to catch Jesus and His disciples in an act of violating the letter of the Law. What did the disciples do to arouse their anger (12:1-2)?

_____

_____

_____

b. What did Jesus tell the Pharisees (12:3-7)?

_____

_____

_____

c. What was His main point?

_____

_____

_____

12. a. In 11:27 Jesus stated that all things had been committed to him by the Father; therefore He could speak authoritatively on the issue of the Sabbath. In 12:8, who does He say is Lord of the Sabbath?

_____

_____

For Further Study:
Read 1 Samuel 21:1-6 and Numbers 28:9-10. What do these two passages teach us? What should the Pharisees have realized?

b. What does He mean?

_____

_____

_____

13. a. What "trick" question did the Pharisees ask Jesus (12:10)?

_____

_____

_____

b. How did Jesus answer their question?

_____

_____

_____

14. a. How did the Pharisees react when Jesus healed the man in 12:13?

_____

_____

_____

b. By recounting this incident, what does Matthew intend for us to know?

_____

_____

_____

For Further Study:
Read Isaiah 42:1-9.
What does the full context of this passage reveal about the Servant to come? How does Jesus fit this revelation?

God's chosen servant (12:15-21)

15. Why did Jesus withdraw from the synagogue (12:15)?

_____

_____

_____

_____

16. a. How did Jesus respond to those who followed Him (12:15-16)?

_____

_____

_____

_____

b. What warning did He give them? Why?

_____

_____

_____

_____

17. a. Why does Matthew quote Isaiah (12:17-21)?

_____

_____

_____

b. What does it confirm about Jesus?

_____

_____

_____

_____

92

Your response

18. List any questions you still have about this lesson.

_____

_____

_____

_____

_____

_____

For the group

Warm-up. Begin this lesson by imagining that you're a car that runs on emotional, physical, and spiritual fuel. On a scale of 0 to 10 (0 = empty; 10 = full), how full is your tank today?

Prayer. As you close this lesson in prayer, thank God for the promises He gives us. Think if there is an area in your life where you need the rest and comfort Jesus offers. Pray that you will remember His promise during those times when you feel particularly weary and need rest.

Matthew 12:22-50

Evidence of Christ's Claims

What evidence could Jesus give to back up His extraordinary claims that He was God? Just one: Jonah spent three days and nights in the belly of the fish, so Jesus would spend three days and nights in the heart of the earth. If His opponents insisted on proof, they would have to wait. But already the events that would lead to that proof had been set into motion.

Jesus and Beelzebub (12:22-37)

1. a. What does Jesus do for the man brought to Him in 12:22?

_____

_____

_____

_____

b. What question did Jesus' actions prompt among the people?

_____

_____

_____

2. a. To whom did the Pharisees ascribe Jesus' power (12:24)?

_____

_____

b. In whose power does Jesus say He performed these miracles?

_____

_____

3. Why is it impossible for Satan to drive out the demons, according to Jesus (12:25-27)?

_____

_____

_____

_____

4. Jesus clearly states that every person must make a decision. What sort of decision is this (12:30)?

_____

_____

_____

_____

5. a. What kinds of sins will be forgiven (12:31-32)?

_____

_____

_____

b. Which ones will not? Why?

_____

_____

_____

Blasphemy against the Spirit (12:31). Ascribing to Satan that which is of the Holy Spirit.

6. a. How are our actions like "fruit" (12:33)?

_____

_____

_____

b. In what way will we be judged?

_____

_____

_____

7. a. When we think of judgment, we most often think of our actions. What does Jesus say about the tongue and the words we speak?

_____

_____

_____

b. According to Him, where do our words come from (12:36-37)?

_____

_____

_____

_____

c. Does this passage comfort you or convict you? Explain.

_____

_____

_____

_____

Optional Application:
If someone had secretly recorded and listened to your words spoken in "secret" this past week, what would they have heard? How do these words reflect your true character? What can you do to get a better handle on the words you speak?

For Further Study:
Read James 1:26, 3:2-12. What do you learn about the "tongue" in these passages? What insights do they give you? What instructions? What warnings? What encouragement?

The sign of Jonah (12:38-45)

8. a. Who asked for a miraculous sign from Jesus (12:38)?

_____

_____

_____

b. What was the reason for this request?

_____

_____

_____

c. How did Jesus respond (12:39)?

_____

_____

_____

9. What is the "sign of the prophet Jonah" (12:39)?

_____

_____

_____

_____

10. Did the Pharisees realize that this sign was evidence for the claims Jesus made in 11:1–12:21?

_____

_____

_____

_____

11. If you had been listening to Jesus' conversation with the Pharisees, would this evidence have satisfied your curiousity about Jesus' true identity? Why or why not?

_____

_____

_____

_____

_____

12. a. What comparison does Jesus make between Jonah and Himself (12:40)?

_____

_____

_____

b. How does Jonah provide a picture of what would happen to Jesus?

_____

_____

_____

Nineveh (12:41). The capital of the old Assyrian Empire, one of the bloodiest and cruelest empires ever to exist.

13. a. How were the men of Nineveh saved from judgment (12:41-42)?

_____

_____

_____

_____

b. By implication, how does Jesus suggest His own audience could be saved?

_____

_____

_____

_____

c. How is the sin of Jesus' audience greater than that of Nineveh?

_____

_____

_____

14. a. What do you learn about the behavior of evil spirits from 12:43-45?

_____

_____

_____

b. In what way is this a picture of the generation that confronted Jesus?

_____

_____

_____

Jesus' mother and brothers (12:46-50)

15. a. How did Jesus respond to His mother and brothers (12:46-50)?

_____

_____

_____

_____

b. Why did He respond this way?

_____

_____

_____

_____

16. a. How does Jesus broaden the concept of His "true family" (12:49-50)?

_____

_____

_____

_____

b. What implications does this have for you?

_____

_____

_____

Your response

17. List any questions you have about anything in this lesson.

_____

_____

_____

_____

For the group

Warm-up. As you begin this lesson, talk about our need for solid proof. What evidence convinced you to follow Christ?

101

Discussion. As you share your answers from this week's lesson, make a special note of any questions that remain unclear. Help each other by discussing different answers and opinions. The resources listed on pages 199-201 may help answer the most difficult questions. If you still can't find an answer, write down the question and have someone in the group do some research during the week. Be sure to share any information found at next week's meeting.

LESSON EIGHT

Matthew 13:1-52

Parables
of the Kingdom

One of Jesus' favorite teaching tools was the parable. As
He and His disciples traveled through the countryside,
He would point to the flowers and the farmers and the
birds and the beasts and use them as illustrations to
make spiritual points. This delighted the crowds and
they were eager to hear Him, for they found they could
easily understand His teaching. He did not use the spe-
cialized vocabulary of the theological schools but instead
spoke of spiritual issues in common, everyday terms.
    Most of the time the Master employed parables to
communicate spiritual truths quickly and easily; yet occasionally He also used parables, not to clarify, but to puzzle.
"This is why I speak to them in parables," He told His disciples, "Though seeing, they do not see; though hearing,
they do not hear or understand" (Matthew 13:13). Jesus
used these kinds of parables to sift the genuinely inter-
ested from the merely curious. Those who really wanted
to know the meaning of these puzzling words would pursue the meaning until they found it; those who merely
wanted entertainment would drift away.
    Matthew 13 includes both kinds of parables, and
so offers a condensed and powerful selection of Jesus'
unforgettable teaching.

The parable of the sower (13:1-23)

1. Matthew 13:1-2 tells us that Jesus went out of the
   house where He had been staying and sat by the

103

lake, but He soon changed locations. What did He do, and why?

_____

_____

_____

_____

_____

2. Why did Jesus use parables to teach the crowds (13:3,10-15)?

_____

_____

_____

_____

_____

Rocky places (13:5). Shallow soil on top of solid rock.

3. Jesus' first parable is about a farmer who sowed some seed (13:3-9). What are the elements used to tell the story?

_____

_____

_____

_____

_____

_____

_____

4. a. What was given to the disciples but not to the crowd (13:11)?

_____

_____

_____

_____

b. What is the connection between this and verse 12?

_____

_____

_____

_____

5. a. What special privilege did the disciples have (13:16)?

_____

_____

_____

b. Who had longed to see what the disciples were witnessing?

_____

_____

_____

c. What is significant about Jesus' comment in verse 17?

_____

_____

_____

_____

For Further Study:
Read Isaiah 6:1-13. This is the text Jesus partially quotes in Matthew 13:13-15. What is the context in Isaiah? To whom is the Lord speaking there? How does this relate to the people in Jesus' day?

For Thought and Discussion: Jesus says that those who receive Him and His Word are "blessed." What does He mean? In what ways have you been blessed by Christ and His Word?

6. Jesus gives his own interpretation of the parable of the sower in Matthew 13:18-23. According to Jesus, to what do each of the following refer:

"The seed that fell along the path" _____

_____

_____

_____

"The seed that fell among rocks" _____

_____

_____

_____

"The seed that fell among thorns" _____

_____

_____

_____

"The seed that fell on good soil" _____

_____

_____

_____

The parable of the weeds (13:24-30)

The kingdom of heaven is like (13:24). The phrase used to introduce six of the seven parables in this chapter.

Weeds (13:25). Probably darnel, which looks very much like wheat when it is young, although later it is easily distinguished.

7. a. Another type of "seed" is mentioned in 13:24. What is this other seed?

_____

_____

_____

_____

b. Who sowed it?

_____

_____

_____

For Thought and Discussion: Why is it sometimes difficult to tell the difference between those who believe in Christ and those who do not?(See Acts 26:20, Titus 1:16.)

8. a. What was the farmer doing in 13:25-30 while the weeds were sown?

_____

_____

_____

b. What did the farmer tell his servants to do about the weeds?

_____

_____

_____

c. What will happen to the weeds at harvest time?

_____

_____

_____

The parables of the mustard seed and the yeast (13:31-35)

9. Why did Jesus continue to teach in parables (13:34-35)?

_____

_____

Optional Application:
How has the Holy Spirit
brought about growth in
your own life? How has
the Word of God spoken
to you in recent days
regarding your own
personal growth?

_____

_____

_____

_____

The smallest of all your seeds (13:32). While not
the smallest seed known today, in Palestine during
the time of Jesus, the mustard seed was the smallest seed used by farmers and gardeners. Mustard
plants could reach ten feet in height.

10. What is the connection between the kingdom and
the size of the mustard seed and how it grows
(13:31-32)?

_____

_____

_____

_____

11. a. In what way is the kingdom like yeast (13:33)?

_____

_____

_____

b. What is the main point of this parable?

_____

_____

_____

The parable of the weeds explained
(13:36-43)

12. In 13:36 Jesus leaves the crowd, enters a house,
and is asked by His disciples to explain the parable
of the weeds.

108

a. Who is the sower of the good seed?

_____

_____

_____

b. What is the good seed?

_____

_____

_____

c. What is the field?

_____

_____

_____

d. Who sows the bad seed?

_____

_____

_____

e. Who will be the harvesters and when will the harvest come?

_____

_____

_____

f. What will happen to those things that cause sin and all who do evil?

_____

_____

_____

g. What will happen to the righteous?

_____

_____

_____

For Thought and
Discussion: What does
it cost to follow Christ?
Pray for believers who
live in oppressive coun-
tries where they may
have to pay with their
lives for their faith in
Christ.

The parables of the hidden treasure and the pearl (13:44-46)

13. a. The two short parables in Matthew 13:44-46
teach the same basic lesson. What is this lesson?

_____

_____

_____

b. To what does Jesus liken the kingdom of heaven
in these verses?

_____

_____

_____

_____

Study Skill—Parables

Matthew 13:44-46 contains two classic parables;
they are little stories, not simple comparisons.
When interpreting a parable, keep these guidelines
in mind:
  1. A true parable is like a joke—the story
     has one main point that the hearer should
     catch at once. Jesus sets up an ordinary
     situation, then gives it an unexpected
     twist to make His point.
  2. A parable is not meant to be a riddle or
     puzzle with a hidden meaning. Instead,
     just as you are meant to get the point of
     a joke and respond with laughter and per-
     haps a change of heart, so the point of a
     parable should hit you at once, startle you
     into looking at things differently, and
     move you to respond.
  3. In order to "get" a joke about a traveling
     salesman, you have to know something
     about the culture. Likewise, in order to get
     the point of a parable, you have to under-
     stand relevant parts of Jewish culture.
  4. Most parables are not allegories, where

---

every element has symbolic meaning. Rather, a parable has "points of reference"[1] on which the story hinges and a single "point" that calls for a response.[2] The points of reference are chosen to draw the audience into the story so that they will respond when they get the point.

For instance, in Matthew 13:44, the points of reference are the treasure (the kingdom of heaven) and the man (a believer). The parable startles the hearer and demands a response: the kingdom is so valuable that it deserves our very best. For us, the question is, "Do I value the kingdom of heaven above everything else? Do I see it as an incomparable treasure?"

Optional Application:
What areas in your own life are difficult for you to "give up"? Why? What can you do this week to move toward freedom in these areas?

For Further Study:
Read the story of the rich, young ruler in Matthew 19:16-26. What was he asked to give up? Why? Does Jesus' request change from person to person? What might He request of you?

The parable of the net (13:47-52)

14. What does the parable of the net tell us about the judgment to come (13:47-50)?

_____

_____

_____

_____

_____

Optional Application:
Since Jesus is clear about what will happen to the ungodly (see Matthew 13:49-50), list areas where you can be more daring in your effort to reach others with the gospel. What do you intend to do about these areas this week? This month? This year?

15. a. How did the disciples respond to Jesus' question in 13:51?

_____

_____

_____

b. How did Jesus respond?

_____

_____

_____

111

c. What was His point?

_____

_____

_____

Your response

16. List any questions you have about anything in this lesson.

_____

_____

_____

_____

For the group

Warm-up. Begin this lesson by sharing one of your favorite books or stories from childhood. Why is it memorable for you?

Discussion. Parables are still an effective way to communicate truth. Have you ever used parables to share the gospel? If so, what was the response? If not, which parable from this lesson do you think would work best? Why?

Prayer. Close this week's lesson by thanking God that "your eyes . . . see, and your ears . . . hear." Pray that He will continue to reveal His truth in ways you can understand, and that He would show you how to tell others about that truth. Share any prayer requests you might have and pray for each other.

1. Gordon D. Fee and Douglas Stuart, _How to Read the Bible for All Its Worth_ (Grand Rapids, Mich.: Zondervan Corporation, 1982), p. 127.
2. Fee and Stuart, p. 126.

Matthew 13:53–16:12

The Rejection of Christ

Centuries before Jesus' day, Isaiah 53:3 prophesied that the Messiah would be "despised and rejected by men." Now Matthew shows his readers how that prophecy was fulfilled.

Beginning with an incident in Jesus' hometown of Nazareth where the people "took offense at him," Matthew describes how the religious leaders of the day — especially the Pharisees and Sadducees — progressively grew in their opposition to the Messiah, eventually asking for a sign from heaven that would prove His claims. Jesus responds to their demand by reiterating that the only sign they would receive would be the sign of Jonah (see Matthew 12:38-40).

In the midst of His rejection by the Jewish leadership, Jesus once more responds to the faith of a Gentile — this time a Canaanite woman who begs Him to heal her daughter. It is a curious fact that in a book clearly written for Jewish readers, it is Gentiles who most consistently demonstrate faith.

A prophet without honor (13:53-58)

1. a. Why were the people of Jesus' hometown "amazed" at Him?

_____

_____

113

For Thought and Discussion: What did Jesus mean when He said that "only in His own home town and in his own house is a prophet without honor" (13:57)? Is this principle still valid today? If so, describe any examples you think of.

b. What questions did they ask about Him?

John the Baptist beheaded (14:1-12)

Herod the tetrarch (14:1). Herod Antipas, one of the sons of Herod the Great. He ruled over one-fourth of his father's kingdom, Galilee. Matthew also calls him "king," as does Luke, because that was his popular name in Rome (see 14:9).

Herodias (14:3). Herodias was married to her uncle, Herod Philip, who lived in Rome. While Herod Antipas was a guest in their home, he persuaded Herodias to leave her husband and marry him.

2. a. When Herod heard the reports of Jesus' ministry and teaching, who did he think Jesus was (14:1-2)?

b. Why do you think he jumped to this conclusion?

3. a. What had Herod done to John the Baptist (14:3-4)?

114

b. Why had he not killed him (14:5)?

_____

_____

4. a. How did Jesus hear about John's death?

_____

_____

_____

b. How did He react (14:13)?

_____

_____

_____

5. a. Why do you think Jesus chose "a solitary place" for a private retreat after He heard about John's death?

_____

_____

_____

b. Do His actions suggest a pattern for us? Explain.

_____

_____

Jesus feeds the five thousand (14:13-21)

6. a. According to Matthew 14:13, Jesus' private retreat was short-lived. What happened?

_____

_____

_____

115

Optional Application:
How have you responded with compassion to someone in need? List areas where you need to become more sensitive. What can you do about those areas?

b. How did He react (14:14)?

_____

_____

c. What implications does His response have for us?

_____

_____

_____

7. a. What happened when evening approached (14:15)?

_____

_____

b. How did the disciples respond?

_____

_____

c. How did Jesus answer them (14:16)?

_____

_____

_____

d. How might you have responded had you been one of the disciples? Why?

_____

_____

_____

8. a. How much food did the disciples start with (14:17)?

_____

_____

_____

b. What did Jesus instruct them to do with it (14:18)?

_____

_____

_____

c. What did Jesus do with the food they brought Him (14:19)?

_____

_____

_____

d. How much food was left over (14:20-21)?

_____

_____

_____

9. a. What did Jesus want His disciples to learn from this object lesson?

_____

_____

_____

b. What does He want us to learn from it?

_____

_____

_____

Jesus walks on water (14:22-36)

The fourth watch (14:25). According to Roman reckoning, from 2 a.m. to 6 a.m. The Jews had only three watches of the night.

10. a. After performing the great miracle of multiplying the loaves and fish, Jesus told His men to go to the other side of the lake (14:22). What did He do in the meantime (14:23)?

_____

_____

_____

b. Why is this significant?

_____

_____

_____

11. a. What frightened the disciples, who were seasoned sailors?

_____

_____

_____

b. What did Jesus say to them?

_____

_____

12. a. Once Peter realized it was Jesus, what did he request (14:28-31)?

_____

_____

_____

b. What happened?

_____

_____

_____

118

13. a. What significant confession did the disciples make after this event (14:33)?

_____

_____

_____

b. What did they do?

_____

_____

_____

Gennesaret (14:34). "Either the narrow plain, about four miles long and less than two miles wide, on the west side of the Sea of Galilee near the north end (north of Magdala), or a town in the plain. The plain was considered a garden spot of Palestine, fertile and well-watered."[1]

---

14. After the incident with Peter on the lake, what happened next (14:34-36)?

_____

_____

_____

_____

Clean and unclean (15:1-20)

The tradition of the elders (15:2). In Jesus' day, a collection of oral traditions about how to interpret and handle the Mosaic law. The tradition began after the Babylonian captivity when rabbis began to make meticulous rules governing the daily life of the nation.

119

15. a. In Matthew 15:1-9 the Pharisees and teachers of the Law are once again out to catch Jesus and His disciples in an infraction of the Law. Of what is Jesus accused in this passage (15:2)?

_____

_____

_____

_____

b. How does He reply?

_____

_____

_____

_____

16. a. How did the Pharisees react to Jesus' object lesson (15:12)?

_____

_____

_____

_____

b. Do you think Jesus' reply was any less likely to "offend" His critics (15:13-14)? Explain.

_____

_____

_____

_____

The Canaanite woman (15:21-28)

Tyre and Sidon (15:21). Gentile cities on the Mediterranean coast about thirty and fifty miles respectively from Galilee.

17. a. Matthew 15:21-28 tells the story of Jesus' encounter with a Canaanite woman in the region of Tyre and Sidon. What was her problem?

_____

_____

_____

b. How did the disciples react to her?

_____

_____

_____

c. How did Jesus initially react?

_____

_____

_____

d. What explains this behavior?

_____

_____

_____

18. a. What was responsible for Jesus' change in attitude (15:27-28)?

_____

_____

_____

b. How can this incident give us confidence in approaching the Father in prayer?

_____

_____

_____

Jesus feeds the four thousand (15:29-39)

19. a. Before feeding the four thousand, Jesus performed many other miracles (15:30-31). List
them, and describe how the crowd reacted.

_____

_____

_____

_____

b. Why do you think Matthew includes this list of
miracles?

_____

_____

_____

_____

Pharisees and Sadducees (16:1-12)

20. a. Jesus left in a boat for the region of Magadan, the
home town of Mary Magdalene. Once again, the
Pharisees and the Sadducees seek Jesus. What
did they request (16:1)?

_____

_____

_____

_____

b. How did Jesus reply?

_____

_____

_____

_____

21. a. What picture does Jesus use to show them the hardness of their hearts (16:2-4)?

_____

_____

_____

Optional Application: Confess your own areas of little faith, and think of ways to increase your faith. Complete the following sentence: The area where I need greater faith is . . . .

b. How does He describe the kind of generation that asks for a sign?

_____

_____

_____

c. Can our own generation learn from His comment here? If so, how?

_____

_____

22. a. Jesus warns His disciples against what He calls "the yeast of the Pharisees and Sadducees" in 16:5. What does He mean (16:12)?

_____

_____

b. What did the disciples think He meant (16:7)?

_____

_____

c. How does Jesus respond to their discussion in 16:8? Why this reaction?

_____

_____

_____

For the group

Warm-up. Begin this lesson by thinking of a time when you faced opposition, risk, or uncertainty in your life. How did you feel and act in that situation?

Discussion. As you answer the questions in this week's lesson, look for ways you can increase your faith in Christ. Pay special attention to the optional question on page 117 about how Jesus multiplies the little things we give Him. Ask God to increase your faith, just as Jesus multiplied one little boy's lunch to feed a crowd of five thousand.

1. *The NIV Study Bible* (Grand Rapids, Mich.: Zondervan Bible Publishers, 1985), p. 1464.

Matthew 16:13–17:23

The Transfiguration

The disciples did not notice the change, but by this point in Jesus' ministry a decisive shift had occurred. The Master's march to the cross had begun.

But before the end comes, Jesus gives His followers a brief glimpse of His coming kingdom. In the Transfiguration the disciples witness a small slice of the life that awaits them.

Peter's confession of Christ (16:13-20)

Caesarea Philippi (16:13). Not the great and beautiful city of Caesarea on the coast of the Mediterranean built by Herod the Great, but a city built north of the sea of Galilee, near the slopes of Mount Hermon.

1. a. In Matthew 16:13 Jesus asks His disciples, "Who do people say the Son of Man is?" How do the disciples answer?

_____

_____

_____

_____

125

For Thought and Discussion: The question of Christ's true identity is still hotly debated around the world. What answers have you heard people give about Christ's identity? How have you responded to these answers?

For Further Study: For more about the foundation of the church, read Ephesians 2:19-22.

b. What do their answers suggest about their understanding of Jesus' identity?

_____

_____

_____

_____

2. a. In 16:15 Jesus gets more direct: "Who do you say I am?" What is Simon Peter's answer?

_____

_____

b. From whom does Jesus say Simon Peter got the answer?

_____

c. What adjective does Jesus use to describe him? Do you think Peter fully understood what he was saying? Explain.

_____

_____

_____

_____

3. a. What new name does Jesus give Simon (16:18)?

_____

_____

b. What significance is attached to Simon's new name and confession?

_____

_____

_____

_____

126

4. Compare Jesus' words to Peter in 16:19 to His words to all the disciples in 18:18-20. What is His main point in each passage?

16:19	18:18-20

5. a. What warning did Jesus give His disciples in 16:20?

_____

_____

_____

b. Why would Jesus issue such a warning?

_____

_____

_____

Jesus predicts His death (16:21-28)

6. Jesus tells the disciples about His future in 16:21-23. Why did Jesus respond to Peter's outburst with such force (16:23)?

_____

_____

_____

_____

127

For Thought and Discussion: Sometimes it is difficult to differentiate between God's will and our own. What guidelines can improve our ability to discern God's will? What lessons can you learn from Peter's experience in Matthew 16:21-23?

For Thought and Discussion: Discuss the positive and negative aspects of being a Christian in an open society (like the United States or England). If religious freedom were to disappear in the near future, what do you think would happen to the church? What would happen to your own faith? Why?

7. a. In 16:24 Jesus explains the cost of following Him. What does He say we must do to be His followers?

_____

_____

_____

b. How can we do this today?

_____

_____

_____

_____

8. a. What is the value of a person's soul (16:26)?

_____

_____

_____

b. In what way is His question really a warning? How is this warning especially applicable to those who live in an affluent society?

_____

_____

_____

9. How does 16:27 relate to denying oneself, taking up the cross, and following Jesus?

_____

_____

_____

_____

_____

10. What does Jesus mean by the promise He gives in 16:28?

_____

_____

_____

_____

_____

The Transfiguration (17:1-13)

11. a. Six days after Jesus' famous exchange with Peter, He takes three of His closest disciples up on "a high mountain." What happened to Jesus while they were there?

_____

_____

_____

b. What is significant about the appearance of Moses and Elijah?

_____

_____

_____

_____

12. a. Whose voice did the disciples hear coming out of the cloud (17:5)?

_____

_____

_____

_____

For Further Study: The Transfiguration gave the three chosen disciples a preview of the coming kingdom. For further details on this remarkable event, read John 17:1-5 and 2 Peter 1:17-18.

For Thought and Discussion: Why was God's voice important to the Transfiguration? How would the account have changed without it?

b. What did it confirm about Jesus' identity?

_____

_____

_____

_____

13. a. How did the disciples react to the voice (17:6)?

_____

_____

_____

_____

b. How is this typical of most first-hand encounters with God throughout Scripture (see Exodus 3:5-6, Isaiah 6:1-5, Daniel 10:4-8, Acts 9:1-7)?

_____

_____

_____

_____

14. What instruction does Jesus again give His disciples in 17:9?

_____

_____

_____

_____

15. a. Who was the "Elijah" who already had returned?

_____

_____

b. Why was the emphasis on Elijah important?

_____

_____

_____

_____

Jesus heals a demon-possessed boy
(17:14-23)

16. a. After Jesus and His disciples came down from the mountain, the crowds gathered around Jesus. What was requested of Jesus (17:14-15)?

_____

_____

_____

b. What had the man already done (17:16)?

_____

_____

17. Why were the disciples unable to drive out the demon (17:19-20)?

_____

_____

_____

_____

18. a. Jesus predicted His death again in 17:22-23. Did the disciples understand Him this time?

_____

_____

_____

For Thought and Discussion: We live in an age of great cynicism about Christ's kingdom. What influences do you see trying to erode people's faith in Christ?

b. How did they react?

_____

_____

_____

_____

For the group

Warm-up. Begin this lesson by talking about why God was pleased with Jesus. Is He pleased with us? Why do you feel that way?

Discussion. As you study this lesson, keep in mind that the disciples were ordinary men. See the Transfiguration through their eyes and imagine their frustration at not having enough faith to heal the demon-possessed boy. As you see the events in Matthew through their eyes, notice how incredible Jesus' life on earth really was.

Matthew 17:24–18:35

Life in the Coming Kingdom

Jesus was not content merely to give the disciples a glimpse of the coming kingdom in the Transfiguration, He also wanted to give them instruction on the nature and rules of conduct for that kingdom. In chapter 18 He describes the character of those who will populate His kingdom. While subsequent events will make it clear that they understand little of the instruction, Jesus knows that the day will arrive when His teaching will bear fruit in the disciples' lives.

The temple tax (17:24-27)

Two-drachma tax (17:24). An annual temple tax required of every male twenty years of age and older. It was worth about two days' wages and was used to maintain the temple.

1. a. After Jesus and His disciples arrived in Capernaum, tax collectors came to Peter. What did they ask him?

_____

_____

_____

133

b. What was Peter's answer?

_____

_____

2. a. Before Peter even had a chance to tell Jesus what had happened, what did Jesus say to him?

_____

_____

_____

b. What did this reveal about Jesus' knowledge of events outside the realm of His natural senses?

_____

_____

_____

3. a. In your own words, what lesson did Jesus teach Peter in 17:25-27?

_____

_____

_____

b. In what way did he "violate" His own lesson? Why?

_____

_____

_____

The greatest in the kingdom (18:1-9)

4. a. What do you think lay behind the disciples' question (18:1)?

_____

_____

b. What were they really asking?

_____

_____

_____

_____

5. a. What object lesson did Jesus use to answer their question?

_____

_____

_____

b. What must we do to enter the kingdom of heaven (18:2-4)?

_____

_____

_____

6. a. What element(s) of a child's character do you think Jesus had in mind here?

_____

_____

_____

_____

b. What warning does Jesus issue to adults who would cause "these little ones" to sin (18:6)?

_____

_____

_____

_____

For Further Study: The connection between genuine faith and resulting godly behavior frequently appears in Scripture. For just a few examples, see the following: Romans 15:18-19; Hebrews 3:18-19; James 1:26, 2:14,17-18,24; 1 John 4:20; 2 Peter 1:5-11.

For Further Study: Angels are mentioned hundreds of times in the Bible. Get a concordance and do a Scripture study on angels. Or read a good book on angels: For example, *Angels* by Billy Graham or *What the Bible Says About Angels* by David Jeremiah.

7. What kinds of things "cause people to sin" (18:7)?

_____

_____

_____

_____

_____

8. Jesus uses exaggeration to tell us that our behavior matters a great deal to Him and, in fact, has eternal consequences (18:8-9). What is His main point?

_____

_____

_____

_____

_____

The parable of the lost sheep (18:10-14)

9. a. Who watches over the little children?

_____

_____

b. How does this statement relate to Jesus' warning not to look down on children?

_____

_____

_____

10. What does the parable of the lost sheep tell us about God's character?

_____

_____

136

_____

_____

_____

A brother who sins against you (18:15-20)

Church (18:17). Matthew is the only Gospel writer to use this term. He apparently means it in the same way we do, i.e., the local congregation.

For Thought and Discussion: Matthew 18:17 establishes one basis for excommunication. What do you think of excommunication? Do we see much of this kind of church discipline in our churches today? When? Where? (See also 1 Corinthians 5:1-13.)

11. a. There are times when a fellow believer (a "brother") offends us. How does 18:15-16 instruct us to deal with these situations?

_____

_____

_____

_____

b. If, after exhausting all options, a brother does not respond, what does Jesus tell us to do (18:17)?

_____

_____

_____

12. What does Jesus promise in 18:20?

_____

_____

_____

_____

Optional Application:
Meditate on how you
have seen and tasted
Christ's mercy in your
life. What does your
treatment of others say
about you? Is there
someone to whom you
need to extend forgive-
ness and mercy?

The parable of the unmerciful servant
(18:21-35)

13. a. In 18:21 Peter asks Jesus a significant question regarding how we must forgive one another. How many times did Peter think was more than enough?

_____

b. How many times did Jesus say we must forgive?

_____

c. What does this number really suggest?

_____

_____

_____

_____

14. a. To illustrate His teaching on forgiveness, Jesus tells a story about a king's servant who becomes an object of the king's mercy. What is Jesus' point?

_____

_____

_____

b. Do you think we take this point seriously? Explain.

_____

_____

_____

Your response

15. How have you seen mercy shown to others? To you?

_____

138

_____

_____

_____

_____

_____

16. How can you practice mercy this week?

_____

_____

_____

_____

17. List any questions you might have about anything in this lesson.

_____

_____

_____

_____

For the group

Warm-up. As you begin this lesson ask the following questions: Have you ever lost anything valuable? What was it? Did you find it again? If so, how?

Prayer. In the parable of the unmerciful servant, Jesus tells us that we must forgive others in order to be forgiven. Are there people in your life you need to forgive? As a group, talk about the nature of forgiveness and how you've forgiven others (or been forgiven yourself) in the past. Spend time in prayer thanking God for His forgiveness and asking for His help to forgive others who have hurt you. Pray for each other during the week as you seek out those people you need to forgive.

Matthew 19:1–20:34

The Journey to Jerusalem

As Jesus makes His way to Jerusalem—and the cross—He continues to instruct the disciples on a variety of subjects: divorce, the place of children, wealth, service, and seeking honor.

Jesus predicts His death again as He prepares His disciples for the coming events in Jerusalem, and gives them a veiled warning of the suffering and persecution they will face. Throughout this teaching, Jesus continues His healing ministry.

Divorce (19:1-12)

A certificate of divorce (19.7). Deuteronomy 24:1 4 outlines the rules for divorce and remarriage. The Pharisees in Matthew 19 say Moses "commanded" it, but Deuteronomy makes it clear, as Jesus pointed out, that Moses only "permitted" it because of the hardness of the people's hearts.

1. a. When Jesus left Galilee, He went into Judea on the other side of the Jordan. There large crowds followed Him and He healed the sick. But His enemies soon reappeared. What did they do in 19:3?

For Further Study:
Read Genesis 1:27-28,
2:24; Proverbs 5:1-23;
Malachi 2:13-16. What
is God's unequivocal
word about marriage in
these passages? Why do
you think we so often
want to talk about the
extreme cases and the
exceptions, rather than
the ideal?

b. What did they hope to accomplish with this
question?

_____

_____

_____

2. a. How did Jesus confirm God's plan for marriage
(19:4-9)?

_____

_____

_____

b. What is God's ideal plan for marriage?

_____

_____

_____

3. a. Why did Moses permit divorce (19:8)?

_____

_____

_____

b. What one reason does Jesus give for divorce
(19:9)?

_____

_____

_____

4. a. How did the disciples react to Jesus teaching on
marriage, divorce, and remarriage (19:10)?

_____

142

_____

_____

b. How do you react? Why?

_____

_____

_____

_____

For Thought and Discussion: What are some of the effects of the breakdown of marriage on our society? Discuss why marriages are breaking up at a greater rate today.

5. What are some of the advantages and disadvantages of being single (see also 1 Corinthians 7:1-2,6-9,25-35,38)?

advantages	disadvantages

Little children and the rich young man
(19:13-30)

6. a. How did the disciples react to the children brought to Jesus (19:13)?

_____

_____

b. How did Jesus respond?

_____

_____

_____

Easier for a camel to go through the eye of a needle
(19:24). The language is exaggerated to make a point. Some commentators have talked about a small gate in Jerusalem called "the eye of the needle," but this is purely fictitious.

7. A rich man came to Jesus with a burning question. What was it (19:16-22)? Why did Jesus talk to him about who is "good"?

_____

_____

_____

_____

_____

8. a. What did Jesus say the young man had to do to "enter life" (19:17-19)?

_____

_____

_____

b. Which of the commandments did Jesus omit? Why? (See Exodus 20:1-17, Deuteronomy 5:6-21.)

_____

_____

_____

_____

_____

9. a. What did Jesus say the man still lacked?

_____

_____

_____

144

b. What was the man's reaction to this require-
ment? Why?

_____

_____

_____

_____

Optional Application:
Too often we act like the
rich young man. Medi-
tate on the truth of this
passage and identify
areas you are still keep-
ing for yourself. Then
surrender those areas to
Jesus.

10. a. What question do the disciples ask in 19:25?

_____

_____

_____

_____

b. How does Jesus answer them?

_____

_____

_____

_____

11. a. Since the disciples have left everything to follow
Jesus, Peter wonders what their reward will be.
What is Jesus' answer (19:28-30)?

_____

_____

_____

_____

b. In the end, is it really a sacrifice to follow Christ?
Explain.

_____

_____

_____

145

The parable of the workers in the vineyard (20:1-19)

Denarius (20:2). A denarius was the usual pay for a day's work. A Roman soldier received a denarius a day.

---

12. a. Why did the workers in the parable grumble at their payment at the end of the day (20:11-12)?

_____

_____

_____

b. How did the landowner answer them (20:13-15)?

_____

_____

_____

c. How does Jesus' statement about the first and the last relate to this parable?

_____

_____

_____

_____

13. Jesus predicts His death again in 20:17-19. What additional details does He give this time?

_____

_____

_____

_____

A mother's request (20:20-28)

For Further Study:
Read Mark 10:32-34
and Luke 18:31-33.
What additional informa-
tion do these passages
give about Jesus' pre-
diction of His death?
What, in particular, does
Luke add?

The mother of Zebedee's sons (20:20). Mark writes that James and John ask the question (Mark 10:35-45); apparently all three made the request of Jesus.

The cup I am going to drink (20:22). A veiled refer-ence to the crucifixion.

14. a. Why does the mother of Zebedee's sons (James and John) come to Jesus in 20:20-21?

_____

_____

_____

b. What word best describes her motivation?

_____

_____

c. How does Jesus reply (20:22-23)?

_____

_____

15. a. How do the other disciples react to this request (20:24)?

_____

_____

b. What must we become to be great in Christ's kingdom?

_____

_____

147

For Thought and Discussion: How do our own ambitions to be great interfere with our service to the Lord? Relate the story of someone you personally know who exemplifies servanthood.

Optional Application: Jesus' question in Matthew 20:32, "What do you want me to do for you?" can be applied to us today. Think of areas in your own life where you need the touch and healing of Jesus.

Two blind men receive sight (20:29-34)

16. As Jesus and His disciples left Jericho, a large crowd followed (20:29-31). What did the men sitting by the roadside shout to Jesus?

_____

_____

_____

_____

17. a. What did Jesus do for the men?

_____

_____

b. What did the men do after they were granted their request?

_____

_____

For the group

Warm-up. Begin this lesson by telling the group your most prized possession. How would you feel if you had to give it up?

LESSON THIRTEEN

Matthew 21:1–22:46

The Triumphal Entry

As Jesus enters Jerusalem amid the crowd's excitement, who could guess that Gethsemane awaits? See Him mounted on a colt, as the crowds shout, "Hosanna to the Son of David! Blessed is he who comes in the name of the Lord!" And witness His anger at those who defile the temple with illicit profiteering!

Time is winding down and Jesus' teachings reflect that fact. One by one, He silences His opponents in a breathtaking display of scriptural understanding and brute logic. No wonder that when the smoke clears, Matthew reports that "from that day on no one dared to ask him any more questions" (22:46).

The triumphal entry (21:1-11)

Bethphage (21:1). Mentioned only in connection with the triumphal entry of Jesus. The Talmud says only that it is "close" to Jerusalem. The name itself means "house of figs."

1. a. When Jesus and His disciples came to Bethphage on the Mount of Olives, the Savior sent two of His men on a special mission. What was that mission (21:2-3)?

For Further Study:
Read Zechariah 9:9,
Psalm 118:26, Isaiah
62:11. How do these
texts prophesy Jesus' triumphal entry? Do you
think the people at the
time recognized what
was happening? Explain.

b. What was the significance of this action (21:4-5)?

Hosanna (21:9). A transliteration of the Hebrew word
from Psalm 118:25-26 that originally was a cry for
help: "Save!" In time it became "an invocation of
blessing and even an acclamation."[1]

---

2. a. The whole city of Jerusalem was stirred as Jesus
and the crowds entered the city. What was the
crowd's question in 21:10?

b. What answer came back?

Jesus at the temple (21:12-17)

3. Why did Jesus enter the temple area in Jerusalem
(21:12-16)? List at least three reasons for His
action.

150

The fig tree withers (21:18-22)

4. a. On His return to Jerusalem the next day, what did Jesus say to the fig tree (21:18-19)?

_____

_____

b. What happened?

_____

_____

c. What was Jesus' response to this event (21:20-22)?

_____

_____

_____

Jesus' authority questioned (21:23-27)

5. a. What did the chief priests and elders ask Jesus in 21:23?

_____

_____

_____

b. How did Jesus reply (21:24-25)?

_____

_____

_____

c. How did they react to Jesus' question (21:26)?

_____

_____

_____

Optional Application:
Why do we often act like
the two sons in Matthew
21:28-30 when Jesus
calls us to go and work
in the world around us?
What steps can we take
to change?

The parable of the two sons (21:28-32)

6. a. In your own words, recount the parable of
Matthew 21:28-30.

_____

_____

_____

_____

_____

_____

b. What is the main lesson to be learned?

_____

_____

_____

The parable of the tenants (21:33-46)

The tenants (21:34). A veiled reference to the Jews or
their leaders. The servants represent the Old Testament prophets, many of whom were killed. The
son represents Christ who was condemned to
death by the religious leaders. The "other tenants"
refer to the Gentiles to whom Paul turned when
many of the Jews rejected the gospel.

7. a. What question does Jesus ask about His parable
in verse 40?

_____

_____

_____

152

b. What is the reply in verse 41?

_____

_____

_____

_____

8. a. What became clear to the Pharisees as Jesus
explained the parable (21:42-45)?

_____

_____

_____

_____

b. What did they plan to do about it (21:45-46)?

_____

_____

_____

The parable of the wedding banquet
(22:1-14)

9. a. How did the invited guests respond to the king's
invitation?

_____

_____

b. What did they do to the king's servants?

_____

_____

c. What did the king do in return?

_____

_____

For Thought and Discussion: In what ways is Jesus still a "stumbling stone" to many today (Matthew 21:42)? How is He a stumbling stone to your friends? Your neighbors? Your coworkers? To you? If so, how?

10. a. How did one guest in this parable insult his host (22:11)?

_____

_____

b. What was his punishment?

_____

_____

c. Why is this important to the parable?

_____

_____

_____

Questions to trick Jesus (22:15-40)

Herodians (22:16). Supporters of the Roman rule and Herod, they were bitter opponents of the Pharisees, who were ardent nationalists opposed to Roman rule.

Denarius (22:19). The bringing of a denarius to Jesus may have had more significance than it appears at first. On one side of the coin was a portrait of Emperor Tiberius; on the other side an inscription in Latin said, "Tiberius Caesar Augustus, son of the divine Augustus." In distinguishing clearly between Caesar and God, Jesus also taught against the false and idolatrous claims made on the coins.

11. a. How did the Pharisees phrase their question to Jesus(22:16-17)?

_____

_____

_____

_____

154

b. Despite this, what did Jesus know about their intent (22:18)?

_____

_____

c. How did He answer the question about paying taxes?

_____

_____

_____

12. a. Next it was the Sadducees' turn to lay a trap for Jesus. What question did they ask Him (22:23-28)?

_____

_____

_____

b. How did He respond (22:29-32)?

_____

_____

_____

13. a. Hearing that Jesus had silenced the Sadducees, the Pharisees figured they would give it another shot. What did they ask Him this time (22:34-36)?

_____

_____

_____

_____

b. How did Jesus reply (22:37-40)?

_____

_____

Optional Application:
How well are you obey-
ing the Great Com-
mandment? How do
you demonstrate the
first by complying with
the second?

**For Thought and
Discussion:** Why is the
question of Jesus' iden-
tity still relevant? What
can we do to make His
name known? How do
you personally make
Christ known?

Jesus asks a question (22:41-46)

14. a. The rounds of questions came to a halt when
Jesus asked His own question. What does Jesus
ask in 22:41-45?

_____

_____

_____

b. Why did this question so completely silence His
adversaries?

_____

_____

_____

c. What is the only possible answer to His question?

_____

_____

_____

Your response

15. Which of the parables from this lesson convicted
you the most? Why?

_____

_____

_____

_____

_____

16. List any questions you may still have from this
    lesson.

_____

_____

_____

_____

_____

_____

For the group

Warm-up. What celebrity would you stand in a big
crowd for hours to see if he or she came to your town?

Discussion. As you study this lesson, discuss Jesus'
statement in 21:21-22. How do doubts influence your
faith? Is it possible to have the kind of faith Jesus
describes while here on earth? Why, or why not?

Wrap-up. End this lesson by sharing any questions
you still have about this lesson.

1. D. A. Carson, "Matthew" in *The Expositor's Bible Commentary: Volume 8* (Grand Rapids, Mich.: Zondervan Publishing House, 1984),
p. 439.

Matthew 23:1–25:46

Warnings of Judgment

Those who think of Jesus only in terms of the gentle Savior, the meek and humble servant, will not be prepared for Matthew 23. It is one of the most scathing denunciations of religious hypocrisy—and hypocrites—that exists anywhere in literature. In angry tones Jesus pronounces seven "woes" on the Pharisees and teachers of the law, calling them "snakes" and "vipers" and "whitewashed tombs" and asking them, "How will you escape being condemned to hell?"

But anger is not the only emotion the Messiah expresses. His heart is broken because of the hardness of heart He sees all around Him as He weeps for the judgment He knows is coming. As He peers into the future, He describes what lies ahead: the temple devastated, false prophets, famines, earthquakes, marauding armies—in fact, "great distress, unequaled from the beginning of the world until now."

Yet that is not all, for the Messiah Himself will return at that time to claim His kingdom. The disciples love this news, and wonder when it will happen. No one knows the exact time, so the disciples should always be ready.

Seven woes (23:1-39)

Sit in Moses' seat (23:2). Those who are the authorized successors of Moses are the teachers of the Law.

159

For Thought and Discussion: Jesus says that the Pharisees "do not practice what they preach" and that "everything they do is for men to see." Could these statements ever describe us? How can we solve the problem of living differently from our beliefs?

For Further Study: Read Numbers 15:37-41 and Deuteronomy 6:8, the texts that inspired the tassels and phylacteries. What was the original intent of these commands?

Phylacteries (23:5). Boxes containing Scripture verses worn by pious Jews on their foreheads and arms. The Scriptures came from four passages, Exodus 13:1-10,11-16; Deuteronomy 6:4-9; and Deuteronomy 11:13-21.

1. a. According to Matthew 23:1-4, what does Jesus tell the crowd regarding the authority of the Pharisees and the teachers of the Law?

_____

_____

_____

b. How should the people respond to their *teaching* and *actions*?

Teaching_____

_____

_____

Actions_____

_____

_____

2. a. Jesus pronounces seven "woes" upon the teachers of the law and the Pharisees in 23:13-36. List each one below and why Jesus mentions it.

23:13-14_____

_____

_____

_____

23:15_____

_____

_____

_____

23:16-22 _____

_____

_____

_____

23:23-24 _____

_____

_____

_____

23:25-26 _____

_____

_____

_____

23:27-28 _____

_____

_____

_____

23:29-36 _____

_____

_____

_____

For Thought and Discussion: If Jesus were suddenly to appear on the American church scene today, do you think He might pronounce any "woes" upon it? If so, what might they be?

b. What do these "woes" all have in common?

_____

_____

_____

_____

3. a. Matthew 23:16-22 talks about foolish "oath swearing." How did the "blind guides" distort the Bible's teaching here?

_____

_____

_____

b. What did it really mean when someone swore by the "altar," the "temple," or "heaven"?

_____

_____

_____

4. a. According to 23:23, what is more important than tithing?

_____

_____

_____

b. What should the people have done both in regard to tithing and "the more important matters of the law"?

_____

_____

_____

_____

5. a. Go back through Matthew 23:13-36 and list the various pictures Jesus uses to describe the Pharisees and the teachers of the law.

_____

_____

_____

_____

b. Why does the Lord describe these men in such pejorative terms? (Is He just venting, or does He want something to happen?)

_____

_____

_____

_____

Signs of the end (24:1-35)

Not one stone left upon another (24:2). This prophecy was fulfilled in A.D. 70. The Romans under Titus completely destroyed Jerusalem and the temple buildings. Stones were even pried apart to collect the gold leaf that melted from the roof when the Temple was set on fire.

The abomination that causes desolation (24:15). The prophet Daniel spoke of the desolation of the temple and Jerusalem in Daniel 9:26-27. This prophecy was at least partially fulfilled in A.D. 168 when Antiochus Epiphanes erected a pagan altar to Zeus on the sacred altar in the temple in Jerusalem. Many people believe that the complete fulfillment of this prophecy will not occur until shortly before Christ's return.

6, a. According to 24:1, to what did the disciples call Jesus' attention?

_____

_____

_____

b. How did He reply?

_____

_____

_____

For Further Study:
Read Genesis 4:8 and 2 Chronicles 24:20-22 regarding the deaths of Abel and Zechariah[1], as mentioned by Jesus in Matthew 23:35.

Optional Application:
Some of the saddest words in Jesus' comment on Jerusalem are these: ". . . but you were not willing." Are there any areas in your own life where you "are not willing"? Asking God to show you any areas of unwillingness and change your heart.

163

For Further Study:
Jesus says that "he who stands firm to the end will be saved." This theme of perseverance is a common one throughout Scripture. See 1 Corinthians 15:1-2; Colossians 1:21-23; 1 Timothy 4:16; Hebrews 3:14; Revelation 2:7,11,26-28.

For Thought and Discussion: Jesus says in Matthew 24:14 that the gospel must be preached "in the whole world." What part can you play right now in this great enterprise? What are you willing to sacrifice in this respect?

7. a. What is significant about Jesus' initial response (24:5)?

_____

_____

_____

b. Why is this warning repeated throughout Jesus' response (24:11,23-26)?

_____

_____

_____

c. What does this indicate about the future?

_____

_____

_____

8. a. List the characteristics of the time Jesus describes in 24:6-14.

_____

_____

_____

_____

b. How do you react to this description? Why?

_____

_____

_____

9. According to Jesus, what must happen before the end comes (24:14)?

_____

_____

_____

_____

10. a. In 24:15-22, Jesus describes a time of unparalleled disaster. How does He instruct people to react to it?

_____

_____

_____

b. What promise is given in verse 22?

_____

_____

_____

11. What is the one sure sign of Christ's coming, according to verse 29?

_____

_____

_____

_____

_____

_____

12. a. How does Jesus describe His return (24:29-31)?

_____

_____

_____

For Thought and
Discussion: Describe
what you know about
the "days of Noah" (see
Genesis 6). How are our
own times similar to the
time of Noah? How are
they different? How
should we respond to
these difficult times?

b. How does this description contrast with what
went before?

_____

_____

_____

No one knows that day or hour
(24:36-51)

13. Jesus talks about the timing of these events in two
sections, in 24:32-35 and 24:36-44. In what way is
the second section all too often ignored today?

_____

_____

_____

_____

_____

14. a. What pictures does Jesus use to describe the timing of His coming (24:36-44)?

_____

_____

_____

b. What is His main point?

_____

_____

_____

15. a. What is the main lesson of the story Jesus tells in
24:45-51?

_____

_____

_____

b. What function does the threat in verse 51 serve?

_____

_____

_____

Parables of the Lord's return (25:1-30)

16. In your own words, retell the story Jesus develops in 25:1-13. What is the main point?

_____

_____

_____

_____

_____

_____

Talent (25:15). First used to signify a unit of weight (about seventy-five pounds), then for a unit of coinage.

17. Read through yet another parable about the Lord's return in Matthew 25:14-30. Do you identify with anyone in the story? If so, with whom? Why?

_____

_____

_____

_____

_____

Optional Application:
How often do you meditate on the truth that none of us knows when the Lord will return? How do you obey the Lord's command to "keep watch"? What are some practical steps you can take to keep watch?

Optional Application:
Think about the gifts and talents God has given to you. What are those talents, and how are you using them for Christ's kingdom?

18. a. What is the main point of the parable in 25:14-30?

_____

_____

_____

_____

b. Why do you think that this story also ends with a warning?

_____

_____

_____

_____

_____

The sheep and the goats (25:31-46)

19. a. The narrative in 25:31-46 is not a parable, but a stylized description of future events. What will happen when Christ comes in His glory?

_____

_____

_____

_____

b. Who do the sheep and goats represent?

Sheep_____

_____

Goats_____

_____

168

20. a. What will Jesus say to those on His right (25:34-36)?

_____

_____

b. How will they reply (25:37-39)?

_____

_____

c. What is Jesus' response to them (25:40)?

_____

_____

Judgment

Most evangelicals generally hold one of two inter-pretations of the judgment spoken of in Matthew 25:31-46:

1. It will occur at the beginning of an earthly mil-lennial kingdom (25:31,34). Its purpose will be to determine who will be allowed to enter the kingdom. The criterion for judgment will be the kind of treatment shown to the Jewish people, "these brothers of mine" (verse 40) during the Great Tribulation (25:35-40,42-45). Ultimately, how a person treats the Jewish people will reveal whether or not a person is saved (25:41,46).

2. The judgment occurs at the Great White Throne at the end of the age (Revelation 20:11-15). Its purpose will be to determine who will be allowed to enter heaven and who will be consigned to eternal punishment in hell (Matthew 25:34,46). The basis for judg-ment will be whether love is shown to God's people (see 1 John 3:14-15).

---

21. a. What will Jesus say to those on His left (25:41-43)?

_____

_____

b. How will they reply (25:44)?

_____

_____

c. What is Jesus' response (25:45)?

_____

_____

d. What will be their punishment?

_____

_____

For the group

Warm-up. If you knew for a fact that Jesus would return five years from today, how would you live differently?

Discussion. As you work through this lesson, look for specific instructions about how we should live as we await Christ's return. Take time to address any unanswered questions from this lesson.

Prayer. Spend a few minutes to close in prayer. Pray that God will help you live lives worthy of Him as we wait for the Second Coming. Thank Him that He will return and that He always fulfills His promises. Ask Him for the strength and perseverance to be ready for that day and hour when He appears.

1. D. A. Carson, "Matthew" in *The Expositor's Bible Commentary, Volume 8* (Grand Rapids, Mich.: Zondervan Publishing House, 1984), pp. 485-486.

Matthew 26:1-75

Jesus' Arrest and Trial

Matthew's account of the Savior's arrest and trial has several unique features. Matthew is the only one of the Gospel writers to report that Jesus called Judas "friend" at the time of His arrest in Gethsemane. He is the only one who records Jesus' words in the garden, "Do you think I cannot call on my Father, and he will at once put at my disposal more than twelve legions of angels?"

The plot against Jesus (26:1-5)

1. In Matthew 26:1-3 Jesus once more tells the disciples that He will be put to death. From this account, how do we know that His death is very near?

_____

_____

_____

_____

_____

2. a. Who plotted to kill Jesus?

_____

_____

For Further Study: Read Exodus 12:1-27 to learn why the Passover was celebrated. What parallels do you see here with Jesus' death? In what way was He the ultimate Passover Lamb (see also 1 Corinthians 5:7)?

_____

_____

b. What kept them from doing it during the Passover?

_____

_____

_____

Jesus anointed at Bethany (26:6-13)

3. a. Who comes to see Jesus in Bethany?

_____

_____

b. What did she do?

_____

_____

_____

c. What was significant about her action?

_____

_____

_____

4. a. How did the disciples react to the woman's gesture?

_____

_____

_____

b. How did Jesus respond to them?

_____

_____

172

The Lord's Supper (26:14-35)

For Thought and Discussion: What does it mean to you that Jesus was betrayed from within His own ranks? Even though Jesus knew it would happen (see John 6:64), how do you think He felt when it did?

Thirty silver coins (26:15). Equivalent to 120 denarii. Most workers received one denarius for a day's work.

5. Judas Iscariot is never mentioned in Scripture without the notation that he was the one who betrayed Jesus. How does 26:14-16 describe his preparations for this despicable act?

_____

_____

_____

_____

6. a. How did Jesus instruct His disciples to prepare the Passover (26:17-19)?

_____

_____

_____

b. What is significant about His statement, "My appointed time is near" (26:18)?

_____

_____

_____

c. Do you think the disciples understood His meaning? Explain.

_____

173

_____

_____

The Feast of Unleavened Bread

The first day of the Feast of the Unleavened Bread
fell on 14 Nisan (also called the preparation of the
Passover). The Passover meal was eaten on the
evening of the fourteenth after sunset, therefore
technically on the fifteenth, since the Jewish day
ended at sunset. The Feast of the Unleavened Bread
lasted seven days, from 15 to 21 Nisan. In the time
of Christ, the entire period of Nisan 14-21 was
referred to under that name. Read Leviticus 23:5-6
and Mark 14:12 for further information.

7. How did the disciples react to Jesus' statement in
   26:21?

_____

_____

_____

_____

8. Matthew doesn't note it, but Judas was dismissed
   from the meeting before the Lord's Supper took
   place (see John 13:27-30). Why?

_____

_____

_____

_____

9. a. What significance does Jesus give to the bread?

_____

_____

b. What significance to the cup?

_____

_____

10. a. After the Last Supper, Jesus and His disciples went to the Mount of Olives. What did Jesus predict (26:31-35)?

_____

_____

_____

_____

h. Peter also made a declaration, as did the other disciples. What is it?

_____

_____

_____

For Further Study:
Read 1 Corinthians 11:23-30. What does the Apostle Paul say about the purpose of celebrating the Lord's Supper? How is this remembrance of Christ meaningful to you?

Optional Application:
All of us, like the disciples, have probably made promises to Christ in the "heat of the battle." What does Deuteronomy 23:21-23 say about our promises (vows) to God?

Gethsemane (26:36-46)

11. a. What instructions did Jesus give the disciples in the garden?

_____

_____

b. What happened?

_____

_____

12. How would you characterize Jesus' emotional state in the Garden of Gethsemane?

_____

175

Optional Application:
Prayer has always been
one of the most difficult
disciplines for Christ's
followers to master.
How is your prayer life?
Identify areas that
cause you to falter in
the area of prayer. What
can you do to rectify
these problems?

13. a. What did Jesus ask His Father?

_____

_____

_____

b. How did this prepare Him for what was to come?

_____

_____

_____

14. How did Jesus' prayer session in the garden conclude (26:46)?

_____

_____

_____

Jesus arrested and tried (26:47-68)

Legion (26:53). A Roman legion contained 6,000 soldiers.

15. a. Who came to arrest Jesus?

_____

_____

_____

176

b. How was Jesus identified for the soldiers who did not know Him?

_____

_____

_____

16. a. Why did Jesus refuse to call on all His available resources (26:54)?

_____

_____

_____

b. How do verses 55-56 illustrate His question in verse 54?

_____

_____

_____

The Sanhedrin (26:59). The high court of the Jews had seventy-one members. Under Roman jurisdiction the Sanhedrin was given great authority, but could not impose capital punishment.

17. a. Those who arrested Jesus took Him to Caiaphas, the high priest, and the other teachers of the law and the elders. What did Peter do (26:57-58)?

_____

_____

_____

b. What did the chief priests and Sanhedrin do? What happened (26:59-61)?

_____

_____

177

For Further Study:
Daniel 7:9-14 provides the key backdrop for Jesus' use of the term "Son of Man." Compare Jesus' words in Matthew 26:64 with Daniel 7:13-14. Do you see why the Jewish religious leaders reacted as they did, since they did not believe Jesus was the Messiah?

_____

_____

_____

_____

18. What did Jesus say in 26:64 that made the high priests charge Him with heresy?

_____

_____

_____

_____

Peter disowns Jesus (26:69-75)

19. a. By whom was Peter challenged about his relationship to Jesus?

_____

_____

_____

    b. When the rooster crowed, what did Peter remember? What did he do?

_____

_____

_____

For the group

Warm-up. Begin this lesson by asking the following questions: "If you were falsely arrested and could make one phone call, who would you call? Why?"

Wrap-up. End this lesson by celebrating the Lord's Supper together as you meditate on the price Christ paid for you at Calvary.

LESSON SIXTEEN

Matthew 27:1-66

The Crucifixion and Burial

Matthew's account of Jesus' death continues to have unique features. His is the only Gospel to tell us what became of Judas the betrayer (although Luke in the book of Acts gives us some further details); the only one to record the words of the people who asked for Jesus to be crucified, "Let his blood be on us and on our children!"; and the only one to report that, upon the Savior's death, the earth quaked and "many holy people who had died were raised to life" and came out of the tombs.

Even in the Savior's death—*especially* in the Savior's death—Matthew wants us to see the power and authority of the Messiah, the Anointed One sent by God.

Judas hangs himself (27:1-10)

Pilate, the governor (27:2). Pontius Pilate served as Governor of Judea under Tiberius Caesar from A.D. 26 to 36. Eventually he was recalled to Rome to answer for brutal tactics used to keep the peace.

Jeremiah the prophet (27:9). The quotation in Matthew seems to combine Zechariah 11:12-13 and Jeremiah 19:1-13, yet Matthew attributes it to Jeremiah only—just as Mark 1:2-3 quotes Malachi 3:1 and Isaiah 40:3 yet attributes the quotation to the major prophet Isaiah alone.

179

1. a. What decision did the chief priests and the elders make regarding Jesus (27:1-2)?

_____

_____

_____

b. Where did they take Him?

_____

_____

_____

2. a. When did Judas feel remorse for what he had done (27:3)?

_____

_____

_____

b. Are remorse and repentance the same thing? Why, or why not?

_____

_____

_____

_____

_____

3. a. How did Judas react when he saw what had happened (27:3-9)?

_____

_____

_____

b. Do you think he expected this? Explain.

_____

"Jeremiah the Prophet"

Read Zechariah 11:12-13 and Jeremiah 19:1-13, the prophecies usually cited in reference to Matthew's comment in Matthew 27:9-10. According to D. A. Carson, "it is fair to say that the quotation appears to refer to Jeremiah 19:1-13 along with phraseology drawn mostly from Zechariah 11:12-13, with the concluding clause a traditional 'obedience formula' used to paraphrase the opening words of Zechariah 11:13. Such fusing of sources under one 'quotation' is not unknown elsewhere in Scripture . . . Jeremiah alone is mentioned, perhaps, because he is the more important of the two prophets, and perhaps also because, though Jeremiah 19 is the less obvious reference, it is the more important as to prophecy and fulfillment."[1]

Jesus before Pilate (27:11-31)

Flogged (27:26). Roman floggings were so brutal that sometimes the victim died before crucifixion.

Praetorium (27:27). The governor's official residence in Jerusalem.

4. a. Since the high priests had no authority to issue a death sentence, they brought Jesus to Pontius Pilate. What did the governor ask Jesus (27:11-14)?

_____

_____

_____

b. What did Jesus do in response to the accusations of the high priests and the elders?

_____

181

_____

_____

5. a. What does the choice of Barabbas over Jesus tell
us about the accusers of Jesus (27:15-18,20-26)?

_____

_____

_____

b. Why does Matthew want us to know about this?

_____

_____

_____

6. a. What message did Pilate receive while he was sitting on the judge's seat?

_____

_____

_____

b. How is this significant?

_____

_____

_____

7. How is the comment of the crowd recorded in 27:25
important to a theme Matthew has introduced several times already (see 21:33-45, 23:37-38, 24:2)?

_____

_____

_____

_____

_____

8. When Pilate realized he had lost control, what did he do (27:26)?

_____

_____

_____

_____

For Thought and Discussion: Pilate asks an important question in Matthew 27:22 — "What shall I do, then, with Jesus who is called Christ?" Why is this question still important? How have you answered the question?

9. a. What did the soldiers do to Jesus in 27:27-31?

_____

_____

_____

b. Why does Matthew include all this detail?

_____

_____

_____

The crucifixion (27:32-56)

A man from Cyrene, named Simon (27:32). Cyrene was an important city of Libya in North Africa that had a large Jewish population. Simon was probably a Jew who was in Jerusalem to celebrate the Passover.

Wine, mixed with gall (27:34). A narcotic painkiller.

10. What happened once the procession arrived at Golgotha (27:35-37)?

_____

_____

_____

_____

For Further Study:
Read the account of
Christ's crucifixion in
Mark 15:21-32, Luke
23:26-43, and John
19:17-27. What similari-
ties do you see? What
differences? Which
account moves you emo-
tionally the most? Why?

11. a. Who was crucified with Jesus (27:38-39,44)?

_____

_____

_____

b. What did they say to Jesus?

_____

_____

_____

12. a. From noon until three o'clock, Matthew tells us
darkness covered the land. What did Jesus cry
out in 27:46?

_____

_____

_____

b. What did the crowd think He said?

_____

_____

_____

c. How did they react (verses 47-49)?

_____

_____

_____

13. a. How do the events of 27:51-53 demonstrate
God's reaction to the crucifixion?

_____

_____

_____

b. How did the centurion and those with him react (27:54)?

_____

_____

_____

_____

The burial (27:57-66)

14. a. Why is it important for Matthew to record Jesus' burial (27:57-61)?

_____

_____

_____

b. Some people believe the women went to the wrong tomb on the Sunday following Jesus' burial. How does verse 61 make that extremely unlikely?

_____

_____

_____

15. a. What concern did the religious leaders express to Pilate (27:62-66)?

_____

_____

_____

b. How did Pilate respond?

_____

_____

_____

Optional Application:
Why was Jesus' death necessary? What does it mean to you personally? Has it changed your life? If so, how? If not, why not?

For Further Study:
Read John 19:38-42 for a fuller description of the burial of Jesus. Note who accompanied Joseph of Arimathea to the tomb. How is this significant?

185

Your response

16. How does studying the crucifixion make you feel? Why?

_____

_____

_____

_____

_____

_____

17. How do you want to respond to the incredible sacrifice Christ made for you?

_____

_____

_____

_____

_____

18. List any questions about this lesson below.

_____

_____

_____

_____

_____

For the group

Warm-up. Begin this lesson by sharing how Christ's death affected your decision to follow Him.

Prayer. Close this lesson by thanking God for sending His only Son to die in your place. Ask for the opportunity to share this incredible gift with others and pray that God will use you to lead others to Him.

1. D. A. Carson, "Matthew" in _The Expositor's Bible Commentary: Volume 8_ (Grand Rapids, Mich.: Zondervan Publishing House, 1984), p. 563.

Matthew 28:1-20

Resurrection!

Judas had betrayed Him, Peter had denied Him, His other disciples had abandoned Him, Caiaphas had condemned Him, Herod had mocked Him, Pilate had tortured and crucified Him—and yet no power on this earth or beyond this earth could keep the Messiah in the grave.

Jesus' crucifixion was not the end, but only the beginning— the beginning of a glorious new chapter in God's dealings with humankind. Hereafter the Son of Man would rule and reign as one to whom "all authority in heaven and on earth" had been granted.

False reports would be spread intending to cover up the truth of His resurrection; yet His disciples would be specially called and empowered to bring the gospel to the ends of the earth, to Jew and Gentile alike.

Nothing would ever be the same again.

The resurrection (28:1-10)

The other Mary (28:1). The wife of Clopas and the sister of Jesus' mother.

1. a. On the first day of the week (after the Sabbath), who went out to look at the tomb (28:1)?

For Thought and Discussion: What can we do to increase our awareness that Jesus is very much alive and that He wants us to know He is ever present with us— despite appearances?

For Further Study: Only Matthew mentions this earthquake and the one at Jesus' death. Read Mark 16:2-6, Luke 24:1-7 and John 20:1 to compare accounts of this event.

_____

_____

b. Where were the men?

_____

_____

_____

2. a. What unusual event took place by the tomb (28:2-7)?

_____

_____

b. What did this visitor look like?

_____

_____

c. How did the guards react to him?

_____

_____

3. a. What did the visitor say to the women?

_____

_____

b. How did the women react to his words?

_____

_____

_____

_____

4. a. What two seemingly contrary emotions filled the women who heard the angel's announcement (28:8)?

_____

_____

_____

b. Have you ever felt these two emotions at the same time? When?

_____

_____

_____

5. a. Who met the women on their way to Galilee (28:9)?

_____

_____

b. How did they react?

_____

_____

_____

c. How do you think you would have reacted? Why?

_____

_____

_____

6. a. What did Jesus tell the women to do (28:10)?

_____

_____

_____

For Thought and Discussion: How has the announcement "he has risen" influenced the world? What did the resurrection prove about Jesus?

Optional Application: What does the resurrected Christ mean to you? How does He affect your day-to-day life?

189

For Thought and
Discussion: What kinds
of doubt are still com-
mon to the followers of
Jesus? How would you
suggest that believers
deal with their doubts?

b. What did He tell them not to do?

_____

_____

_____

The guards' report (28:11-15)

7. a. What did the religious leaders instruct the guards
to say?

_____

_____

_____

_____

b. What reward did they give them for repeating
this story?

_____

_____

_____

c. What has been the result, even to contemporary
times?

_____

_____

_____

8. a. What were the high priests and elders afraid of?

_____

_____

_____

_____

b. What would have happened to Christianity if they
could have produced Jesus' body?

190

For Further Study:
Read Acts 2:38,41 and
Romans 6:3-4. Also read
Romans 8:9-11 and 1
Corinthians 12:13. What
further details do we
learn about baptism in
these texts?

_____

_____

_____

_____

The Great Comission (28:16-20)

Optional Application:
How does The Great
Commission speak to
you personally? Spend
some time in prayer,
considering how the Lord
might want you to
respond to the Great
Commission.

9. a. Where did the eleven remaining disciples go
(28:16)?

_____

_____

_____

b. Verse 17 mentions two contrary actions; what
are these?

_____

_____

_____

10. Matthew 28:19-20 is commonly called "The Great
Commission." How would you state this commission in your own words?

_____

_____

_____

_____

_____

11. a. What promise does Jesus give all of us at the end
of verse 20?

_____

_____

_____

b. How should this change the way we live?

_____

_____

_____

c. Does it? Explain.

_____

_____

_____

For the group

Warm-up. Begin this lesson by talking about how you would have responded if you were one of the women at the empty tomb. How would you feel? How would you describe what happened to the others?

Looking Back

By now you should have a thorough grasp of Matthew's Gospel and be able to explain Jesus' life and teaching to anyone curious about the Christian faith. Right? On the other hand, perhaps you have forgotten a great deal of what you studied in early lessons. A review is the best way to clarify and reinforce what you have learned.

If you can, reread the Gospel of Matthew and glance through the past thirteen lessons. If this sounds like more time than you can afford, a half-hour of reviewing the previous lessons, rereading your completed outline (or the one on pages 21-23), and thumbing through Matthew's Gospel should probably bring back to you the most important things you've learned. Recall from lesson one what you thought the book's main messages were.

As you review the Gospel, answer questions 1-9. Some relevant verses are suggested for each question, but don't feel that you must look at all of these or only these. Also, don't treat the questions like a comprehensive, final exam that requires deep theologizing. Instead, imagine yourself explaining these things to a nonChristian inquirer. Your goal here is to be able to explain the gospel to ordinary people.

1. What new things did you learn about Jesus?

_____

_____

_____

_____

_____

2. What new things did you learn about the kingdom
of God?

_____

_____

_____

_____

3. Which of Jesus' parables struck you most force-
fully? Why?

_____

_____

_____

_____

4. Which of Jesus' non-parabolic teachings influenced
you the most? Why?

_____

_____

_____

_____

5. Did anything Jesus say as recorded in Matthew
offend you? Surprise you? Convict you? Assure
you? Encourage you? Why?

_____

_____

_____

_____

_____

6. What did you learn about Jesus in His many dealings with poor people? With oppressed people?
With sick people? With religious people? With His
own disciples? With His family? What picture finally
emerged for you?

_____

_____

_____

_____

_____

7. Have you noticed any areas (thoughts, attitudes,
opinions, behavior) in which you have changed as a
result of your study of Matthew's Gospel? If so,
describe them.

_____

_____

_____

_____

8. Look back over the entire study at questions in
which you expressed a desire to make some specific
personal application. Are you satisfied with your fol-
low-through? Why or why not? Pray about any of
those areas that you think you should continue to
pursue. Write anything you decide below.

_____

_____

_____

_____

_____

_____

_____

9. Look back over the study at any unanswered questions you wrote down. Have they been answered? If not, make a plan for securing the answers you seek. Perhaps you could start by looking up the needed information in one of the books listed in the Study Aids at the back of this book.

_____

_____

_____

_____

_____

_____

_____

For the group

One way of dealing with a major review is to get a large pad of paper or a markerboard. Beginning with question 1, brainstorm everything you remember about the meaning of the title *Christ*. List the group's thoughts. After about five minutes of brainstorming, summarize the list into a sentence or two of clear, concise definition—something everyone can remember and explain to nonChristians. Then continue to brainstorm and summarize question 2, and so on.

Be sure to save at least ten to fifteen minutes to examine how you've changed (question 7) and how you plan to continue applying what you've learned (question 8). This is a time to encourage and motivate each other to keep going. You may not see dramatic changes in your lives yet; instead, you may see areas you want to continue praying and acting on. Remind the group that God is responsible for results; we are responsible for consistent prayer and trust.

If anyone still has questions about Matthew, plan

ways of finding answers. The sources beginning on
page 199 may help.

Wrap-up. Evaluate how well your group functioned
during your study of Matthew. Some questions you
might ask:

- What did you learn about small group study?
- How well did your study help you to grasp the
  book of Matthew?
- What were the most important truths you dis-
  covered together about God?
- What did you like best about your meetings?
- What did you like least? What would you
  change?
- How well did you meet the goals you set at the
  beginning?
- What are members' current needs? What will
  you do next?

Prayer. Thank God for what He has taught you
through this study. Thank Him for specific ways He is
changing you through your study of Matthew's Gospel.
Thank Him also for your group, and for the freedom to
study the Bible together.

STUDY AIDS

For further information on the material covered in this study, consider the following sources. If your local bookstore does not have them, you can ask the bookstore to order them from the publishers, or find them in a public, university, or seminary library.

Commentaries on Matthew

James Montgomery Boice, *The Sermon on the Mount* (Grand Rapids, Mich.: Zondervan Publishing House, 1972).

A brief, readable treatment on Matthew 5–7 that insists the sermon does several things: it shows the absolute necessity of the new birth, points to the Lord Jesus, indicates the way to blessing for Christians, and shows us how to please our heavenly Father.

D. A. Carson, "Matthew" in *The Expositor's Bible Commentary*, Gen. Ed. Frank E. Gaebelein (Grand Rapids, Mich.: Zondervan Publishing House, 1984).

An easy-to-read, yet thorough treatment of all the major issues in Matthew, whether textual, interpretive, or critical. Interacts well with other sources and provides more technical notes.

Alan Hugh McNeile, *The Gospel According to St. Matthew* (Grand Rapids, Mich.: Baker Book House, reprinted 1980 from an original 1915 edition).

An older, yet valuable work that works from the Greek text. A more technical volume that provides valuable insights.

John F. Walvoord, *Matthew: Thy Kingdom Come* (Chicago: Moody Press, 1974).

This dispensational commentary uses the King James Version as its basis for exposition. Walvoord says Matthew is designed to explain to the Jews—who had expected the Messiah to be a conquering king—why instead Jesus suffered and died, and why His triumph was postponed to His second coming.

Historical sources

F. F. Bruce, *New Testament History* (Doubleday, 1971).
A readable history of Herodian kings, Roman governors, philosophical schools, Jewish sects, Jesus, the early Jerusalem church, Paul, and early gentile Christianity. Well-documented with footnotes for the serious student, but the notes do not intrude.

Alfred Edersheim, *The Life and Times of Jesus the Messiah* (Eerdmans, 1971).
Reprint of the classic two-volume original (second edition) of 1886. Some of the material is out-of-date, but most is still sound. The prose of the life of Jesus is of timeless value. Edersheim was a converted Jew, and his knowledge of the Jewish law makes this book outstanding.

E. F. Harrison, *Introduction to the New Testament* (Eerdmans, 1971).
History from Alexander the Great—who made Greek culture dominant in the biblical world—through philosophies, pagan and Jewish religion, Jesus' ministry and teaching, and the spread of Christianity. Very good maps and photographs of the land, art, and architecture of New Testament times.

Concordances, dictionaries, and handbooks

A *concordance* lists words of the Bible alphabetically along with each verse in which the word appears. It lets you do your own word studies. An *exhaustive* concordance lists every word used in a given translation, while an *abridged* or *complete* concordance omits either some words, some occurrences of the word, or both.

Two of the three best exhaustive concordances are the venerable *Strong's Exhaustive Concordance* and *Young's Analytical Concordance to the Bible*. Both are available based on the *King James Version* and the *New American Standard Bible*. *Strong's* has an index in which you can find out which Greek or Hebrew word is used in a given English verse (although its information is occasionally outdated). *Young's* breaks up each English word it translates. Neither concordance requires knowledge of the original languages.

Perhaps the best exhaustive concordance currently on the market is *The NIV Exhaustive Concordance*. It features a Hebrew-to-English and a Greek-to-English lexicon (based on the eclectic text underlying the NIV), which are also keyed to *Strong's* numbering system.

Among other good, less expensive concordances, *Cruden's Complete Concordance* is keyed to the *King James* and *Revised Versions*, the *NIV Complete Concordance* is keyed to the *New International Version*. These include all references to every word included, but they omit "minor" words. They also lack indexes to the original languages.

A *Bible dictionary* or *Bible encyclopedia* alphabetically lists articles about people, places, doctrines, important words, customs, and geography of the Bible.

The New Bible Dictionary, edited by J.D. Douglas, F.F. Bruce, J.I. Packer, N. Hillyer, D. Guthrie, A.R. Millard, and D.J. Wiseman (Tyndale, 1982) is more comprehensive than most dictionaries. Its 1,300 pages include quantities of information along with excellent maps, charts, diagrams, and an index for cross-referencing.

Unger's Bible Dictionary by Merrill F. Unger (Moody, 1979) is equally good and is available in an inexpensive paperback edition.

The Zondervan Pictorial Encyclopedia edited by Merrill C. Tenney (Zondervan, 1975, 1976) is excellent and exhaustive, and has been revised and updated. Its five 1,000-page volumes represent a significant financial investment, however, and all but very serious students may prefer to use it at a church, public, college, or seminary library.

Unlike a Bible dictionary in the above sense, *Vine's Expository Dictionary of New Testament Words* by W.E. Vine (various publishers) alphabetically lists major words used in the *King James Version* and defines each New Testament Greek word that the KJV translates with its English word. *Vine's* also lists verse references where that Greek word appears, so you can do your own cross-references and word studies without knowing any Greek.

Vine's is a good, basic book for beginners, but it is much less complete than other Greek helps for English speakers. More serious students might prefer *The New International Dictionary of New Testament Theology*, edited by Colin Brown (Zondervan) or *The Theological Dictionary of the New Testament* by Gerhard Kittel and Gerhard Friedrich, abridged in one volume by Geoffrey W. Bromiley (Eerdmans).

A *Bible atlas* can be a great aid to understanding what is going on in a book of the Bible and how geography affected events. Here are a few good choices.

The Macmillan Atlas by Yohanan Aharoni and Michael Avi-Yonah (Macmillan, 1968, 1977) contains 264 maps, 89 photos, and 12 graphics. The many maps of individual events portray battles, movements of people, and changes of boundaries in detail.

The New Bible Atlas by J.J. Bimson and J.P. Kane (Tyndale, 1985) has 73 maps, 34 photos, and 34 graphics. Its evangelical perspective, concise and helpful text, and excellent research make it a very good choice, but its greatest strength lies in outstanding graphics, such as cross-sections of the Dead Sea.

The Bible Mapbook by Simon Jenkins (Lion, 1984) is much shorter and less expensive than most other atlases, so it offers a good first taste of the usefulness of maps. It contains 91 simple maps, very little text, and 20 graphics. Some of the graphics are computer-generated and intriguing.

The Moody Atlas of Bible Lands by Barry J. Beitzel (Moody, 1984), is scholarly, evangelical, and full of theological text, indexes, and references. This admirable reference work will be too deep and costly for some, but Beitzel shows vividly how God prepared the land of Israel perfectly for the acts of salvation He planned to accomplish in it.

A *handbook* of biblical customs can also be useful. Some good ones are *Today's Handbook of Bible Times and Customs* by William L. Coleman (Bethany, 1984) and the less detailed *Daily Life in Bible Times* (Nelson, 1982).

For small group leaders

The Small Group Leader's Handbook by Steve Barker et al. (InterVarsity, 1982). Written by an InterVarsity small group with college students primarily in mind. It includes information on small group dynamics and how to lead in light of them, and many ideas for worship, building community, and outreach. It has a good chapter on doing inductive Bible study.

Getting Together: A Guide for Good Groups by Em Griffin (InterVarsity, 1982).
Applies to all kinds of groups, not just Bible studies. From his own experience, Griffin draws deep insights into why people join groups; how people relate to each other; and principles of leadership, decision making, and discussions. It is fun to read, but its 229 pages will take more time than the above book.

You Can Start a Bible Study Group by Gladys Hunt (Harold Shaw, 1984).
Builds on Hunt's thirty years of experience leading groups. This book is wonderfully focused on God's enabling. It is both clear and applicable for Bible study groups of all kinds.

How to Build a Small Groups Ministry by Neal F. McBride (NavPress, 1994).
This hands-on workbook for pastors and lay leaders includes everything you need to know to develop a plan that fits your unique church. Through basic principles, case studies, and worksheets, McBride leads you through twelve logical steps for organizing and administering a small groups ministry.

How to Lead Small Groups by Neal F. McBride (NavPress, 1990).
Covers leadership skills for all kinds of small groups—Bible study, fellowship, task, and support groups. Filled with step-by-step guidance and practical exercises to help you grasp the critical aspects of small group leadership and dynamics.

DJ Plus, a special section in *Discipleship Journal* (NavPress, bimonthly).
Unique. Three pages of this feature are packed with practical ideas for small groups. Writers discuss what they are currently doing as small group members and leaders. To subscribe, write to Subscription Services, Post Office Box 54470, Boulder, Colorado 80323-4470.

Bible study methods

Braga, James. *How to Study the Bible* (Multnomah, 1982).
Clear chapters on a variety of approaches to Bible study: synthetic, geographical, cultural, historical, doctrinal, practical, and so on. Designed to help the ordinary person without seminary training to use these approaches.

Fee, Gordon, and Douglas Stuart. *How to Read the Bible for All Its Worth* (Zondervan, 1982).
After explaining in general what interpretation and application are, Fee and Stuart offer chapters on interpreting and applying the different kinds of writing in the Bible: Epistles, Gospels, Old Testament Law, Old Testament narrative, the Prophets, Psalms, Wisdom, and Revelation. Fee and Stuart also

suggest good commentaries on each biblical book. They write as evangelical scholars who personally recognize Scripture as God's Word for their daily lives.

Jensen, Irving L. *Independent Bible Study* (Moody, 1963), and *Enjoy Your Bible* (Moody, 1962).
The former is a comprehensive introduction to the inductive Bible study method, especially the use of synthetic charts. The latter is a simpler introduction to the subject.

Wald, Oletta. *The Joy of Discovery in Bible Study* (Augsburg, 1975).
Wald focuses on issues such as how to observe all that is in a text, how to ask questions of a text, how to use grammar and passage structure to see the writer's point, and so on. Very helpful on these subjects.

Titles in the LifeChange series:

7/27/98

Turn your small group from just a bunch of people to a tightly knit community.

Does your small group feel like just a bunch of people? Do you long for greater intimacy and growth?

With Pilgrimage/NavPress Small-Group Training Seminars you can turn your small group into a community of believers excited to study God's Word and apply it to their lives. With new leadership skills and practical "how to" help, you'll be equipped to provide well-trained leadership and direction for your group, turning it from just a bunch of people to a community that supports and cares for one another.

Here's what you'll learn.

You'll learn ►how trends within society set the stage for small groups ►how you can use the four primary phases of group development to guarantee the right fit for every small-group member ►seven ways to cultivate a caring atmosphere ►five common problems to avoid ►the six foundational elements of every small group ►and much, much more!

Space is limited. Call (800) GRPS-R-US today for more information about seminars in your area.

(800) 477-7787, ask for offer **#303**

PILGRIMAGE
NAVPRESS
www.navpress.com

SMALL-GROUP MATERIALS FROM NAVPRESS

BIBLE STUDY SERIES

DESIGN FOR DISCIPLESHIP
GOD IN YOU
GOD'S DESIGN FOR THE FAMILY
INSTITUTE OF BIBLICAL
   COUNSELING Series
LEARNING TO LOVE Series

LIFECHANGE
RADICAL RELATIONSHIPS
SPIRITUAL DISCIPLINES
STUDIES IN CHRISTIAN LIVING
THINKING THROUGH DISCIPLESHIP

TOPICAL BIBLE STUDIES

Becoming a Woman of Excellence
Becoming a Woman of Freedom
Becoming a Woman of Prayer
Becoming a Woman of Purpose
The Blessing Study Guide
Homemaking
Intimacy with God
Loving Your Husband

Loving Your Wife
A Mother's Legacy
Praying From God's Heart
Surviving Life in the Fast Lane
To Run and Not Grow Tired
To Walk and Not Grow Weary
What God Does When Men Pray
When the Squeeze Is On

BIBLE STUDIES WITH COMPANION BOOKS

Bold Love
Daughters of Eve
The Discipline of Grace
The Feminine Journey
Inside Out
The Masculine Journey
The Practice of Godliness
The Pursuit of Holiness

Secret Longings of the Heart
Spiritual Disciplines
Tame Your Fears
Transforming Grace
Trusting God
What Makes a Man?
The Wounded Heart

RESOURCES

Brothers!
Discipleship Journal's 101 Best
   Small-Group Ideas
How to Build a Small-Groups Ministry
How to Lead Small Groups
Jesus Cares for Women
The Navigator Bible Studies
   Handbook

The Small Group Leaders
   Training Course
Topical Memory System
   (KJV/NIV and NASB/NKJV)
Topical Memory System:
   Life Issues